T5-BAH-333

GARLAND STUDIES ON

INDUSTRIAL PRODUCTIVITY

edited by
STUART BRUCHEY
ALLAN NEVINS PROFESSOR EMERITUS
COLUMBIA UNIVERSITY

A GARLAND SERIES

UTILIZING SELF-MANAGING TEAMS

EFFECTIVE BEHAVIOR OF TEAM LEADERS

REBECCA J. KRAFT

GARLAND PUBLISHING, INC.
A MEMBER OF THE TAYLOR & FRANCIS GROUP
NEW YORK & LONDON / 1998

658.4036
K89u

Copyright © 1998 Rebecca J. Kraft
All rights reserved

Library of Congress Cataloging-in-Publication Data

Kraft, Rebecca J., 1952–
    Utilizing self-managing teams : effective behavior of team
leaders / Rebecca J. Kraft.
        p.   cm. — (Garland studies on industrial productivity)
    Includes bibliographical references and index.
    ISBN 0-8153-3210-6 (alk. paper)
    1. Self-directed work teams. I. Title. II. Series.
HD66.K727 1998
658.4'036—dc21
                                                          98-45165

alo

Printed on acid-free, 250-year-life paper
Manufactured in the United States of America

Dedicated to two wonderful people who are my inspiration:
V. Josephine Smith, my mother,
and
David C. Kraft, Ph.D., my husband.
Both are gifted teachers.

University Libraries
Carnegie Mellon University
Pittsburgh PA 15213-3890

Contents

Tables and Figures

Preface

This is a study about the use of self-managing teams in organizations and the effective behaviors of team leaders. In many ways, I began writing and researching this book many years ago. My thought process and line of inquiry is the culmination of fifteen years of learning and experience.

In the early 1980s I becam interested in the newly emerging field of organization development. As I witnessed academics and OD practitioners attempt to define this interdisciplinary field, I also observed the trends in management sciences involved in defining the changing roles of managers. During this time period, I witnessed innovative organizational approaches begin in manufacturing settings and then slowly spread throughout entire organizations.

In the 1990s I was a doctoral student at The George Washington University where I continued to learn about organization design and development. A unique perspective of adult learning theory was introduced to me by Dr. Sharon Confessore as I learned about researchers such as Marsick, Mezirow and Senge. The issue of team leaders as adult learners began to be of interest to me. In addition, Dr. David Schwandt introduced me to the organization theories of Parsons, Weber and Von Bertalanffy. Dr. Marshall Sashkin patiently taught me the art and science of instrument design as he encouraged me to develop my own team leader survey instrument.

Over the course of fifteen years of work experiences and two stints in graduate school, the formation of this research study came to be in 1994. I knew, almost instinctively, that I wanted to research team leaders in self-managing teams from an integrative framework of organization design, adult learning and self-managing teams theory and literature. A summary of the literature review and a discussion of the linkages among the various theories formed the theoretical basis for this study.

While writing this book, I had one foot firmly planted in theory and the other foot in practical applkication in organizations. As a result, the implications of this study for team leader training and development are of primary interest to practitioners. As researchers better define the necessary skills and behaviors of team leaders in self-managing team environments, the organization development and training practitioners may use this information to develop more effective training programs and development activities. In fact, any manager who must select, train, counsel and evaluate team leaders could benefit from the recommendations in this book.

Finally, I believe that organizational leaders must invest time and money far beyond what most consider appropriate today in order to provide conditions in which individuals and teams can develop their capacity to learn and create an organization that they care about. A willingness to invest in creating an environment that helps employees learn and develop is essential to success.

For a career's worth of inspiration, knowledge and friendship, I would like to thank my mentors, Jack Armstrong and Bob Thurston. Finally, I wish to recognize the support and encouragement of my husband, David; without his prodding I would never have embarked upon doctoral studies. Thank-you.

Rebecca J. Kraft
Kansas City
September, 1998

Acknowledgments

I am grateful for the assistance of many helpful people who enabled me to complete this study:

- John L. Armstrong, Jr., who sponsored this research. Without his sponsorship and mentoring, this study would not have been possible.

- The people within the corporation who shared their time with me and completed the survey questionnaires.

- The members of the study committee, especially Marshall Sashkin, chair, who shared his expertise in instrument development, Sharon Confessore for her encouragement, David Schwandt for his confidence, and Sal Paratore for his patience, all faculty of the George Washington University

- Robert H. Thurston, my mentor, who taught me the basics of organization development from his twenty-plus years of practical experience.

Introduction

What is the relationship between team leaders' characteristics and the effectiveness of their teams? That is the central question I sought to answer in this study. Organizations are increasingly using self-managing teams as part of a long-term evolution from traditional hierarchical organizations to flatter, team-based organizations. These self-managing teams occur in a general systems organization context. Although 68% of Fortune 1000 companies report using self-managing teams under the umbrella of employee involvement practices, little empirical evidence is available to show the defining characteristics of successful team leaders or the efficacy of self-managing teams.

This study compared team leadership to team performance in a manufacturing facility of a Fortune 100 company. Data collection methods included two survey instruments completed by team members to assess team leadership. One of these instruments was developed and tested in this study. The same measures of productivity based on performance data were used for all teams.

There were three major findings:

First, the results of the factor analyses of both surveys suggests that the most important aspect of team leadership appears to consist of one broad category of behavior—a general orientation toward empowering others.

Second, a lesser aspect of team leadership emerged which appears to reflect traditional leadership and managerial skills. This suggests that traditional leadership concepts continue to play an important role during the transition to self-managing teams.

Third, the empowered leadership factor was not significantly correlated with the team performance data.

The tenuous relationship between team leadership and team performance is consistent with past research. The results indicate that organizations should proceed cautiously when implementing self-managing teams by ensuring that they put in place the practices that make them effective.

Abbreviations

BRP	Business Resources Planning
BPCS	Business Planning and Control System
SDWT	Self-directed Work Team
SMT	Self-managing Team
SMT Leader Survey	Self-managing Team Leader Survey by Ann Burress ©1994
SMWT	Self-managing Work Team
TLS	Team Leader Survey by Rebecca Kraft c1995

Utilizing
Self-Managing
Teams

CHAPTER 1
Introduction

In recent years, a plethora of advice has been offered on how to create an "excellent," "innovative" or "high performing" organization. Much of this attention has focused on ways to develop the new 1990s organization—one that is global, nonbureaucratic, decentralized, and team-based. The forces causing these massive changes in U.S. corporations include: (1) the global economy, (2) the post-industrial economy, (3) an accelerated pace of change, (4) new demographics, and (5) turnover in corporate control (Eccles, 1992). Similarly, technology, political change and economic change have been cited as having created more complex work in an ever more demanding global business environment (Lawler, 1996).

Researchers have suggested that effective organizations are not only necessary for competitiveness, but provide a growing source for competitive advantage (Galbraith, 1995; Lawler, 1992, 1996). As a result, organizations are experimenting with new work designs to try to increase productivity, quality, innovation and competitiveness in the global marketplace. Some of these organizational forms are known as team-based organizations, lateral organizations, and process management organizations. Recent data collected from Fortune 1000 companies showed that their use of self-managing teams rose from 28% in 1987 to 68% in 1993 (Lawler, Mohrman & Ledford, 1995). These increases are impressive even though the team system was typically used in only a small portion of each company.

The use of teams has been growing for more than 25 years. In the 1960s and 70s, a few manufacturing companies experimented with self-managing teams (Lawler, 1987; Galbraith, 1995). By the early 1990s, this number had grown extensively, evidenced by the number of service organizations, as well as manufacturing organizations, adopting the team approach. As noted above, self-managing work teams gained popularity between 1987 to 1993, and every indication is that they will become even more prevalent (Lawler et al., 1995). Organizations have introduced a variety of teams called empowered teams, cross-functional teams, work teams, quality improvement teams, self-managing teams, or self-directed teams. One of the characteristics of an emerging field is unclear terminology. The word "team" can be traced to the Indo-European word "deuk," which means "to pull," and the word's application to work teams has long meant "pulling together" (Senge, 1990). However, no commonly accepted definition of self-managing teams exists. Researchers at The Center for the Study of Work Teams at the University of North Texas reported documenting more than 30 different terms for work teams (Beyerlein, 1995).

It may seem paradoxical that the term "self-managing" does not mean that direct supervision is absent. Although the role of the self-managing team leader may differ from the role of a traditional supervisor, most self-managing teams have a formal leader who is positioned above the team in the organizational hierarchy (Manz & Sims, 1986). This leader is referred to as an external team leader. In fact, Manz and Sims introduced the topic of leadership as a paradox: How does one lead teams of employees who are supposed to lead themselves? Similarly, Lawler (1996) stated that teams rarely operate effectively without someone or some set of individuals who lead by challenging the group, helping it set priorities and addressing performance problems. By contrast, Galbraith (1995) stated that an emerging view is that teams may not need a formal leader. This view may be especially appropriate for groups with a small number of members and some self-management experience. In these cases, a leader will emerge depending on the issue at hand.

Researchers and practitioners agree that leadership behavior is a key contingency variable in explaining the success or failure of self-managing teams (Ketchum & Trist, 1992; Lawler, 1986; Manz & Sims, 1986, 1987; Mills, 1983; Walton & Hackman, 1986; Wellins & Byham, Wilson, 1991). Lawler (1986) cited the reluctance of supervisors to engage in new behaviors as a major cause of failure in self-managing teams. Similarly, Manz and Sims (1986) indicated that, "In our investigations of self-managed work groups we have found ambiguity and confusion about the role of the appointed external leaders to be the single most troublesome issue of implementation." (p. 144).

Organizational researchers have attempted to determine the specific behaviors required of the external leaders of self-managing teams. A similar question deserving exploration is whether or not these behaviors differ from those required of leaders in traditional groups. Theoretical perspectives on these questions are underdeveloped. Manz and Sims have conducted by far the most serious research on leadership in self-managing teams (Manz & Sims, 1980, 1984, 1986, 1987, 1989, 1993; Manz, Keating, & Donnellon, 1990). According to Manz and Sims (1993), "This new form of leadership also demands a new set of behaviors, which we are only beginning to understand from the emerging research" (p. 3).

PROBLEM STATEMENT

This growth in the adoption of teams has outpaced the ability of theory and research to provide solid underpinnings for sound practices (Mohrman & Cohen, 1994; Manz & Sims, 1993). Although many authors of popular business literature have suggested that using team-based organizations is the key to maintaining organizational effectiveness in these rapidly changing times, little empirical evidence has been generated to support this theory. In fact, so much popular press revolves around team concepts that people may be led to believe that teams provide a universal solution, rather than just being a tool used under appropriate conditions (Galbraith, 1995).

Almost four decades of research has indicated that groups, such as self-managing teams, often exhibit high performance levels and high member quality of work life. Yet many theories are still being used to explain why and under what conditions they are effective (Beekun, 1989; Cohen, 1995; Goodman, Devadas, & Hughson, 1988). This study, therefore, attempted to fill some of the void of empirical evidence by examining the relationship between team leadership and team performance.

PURPOSE OF THE STUDY

The intent of this study was to determine if a relationship exists between team leadership and work team performance and to better define the effective behaviors of team leaders.

A definition of the term "self-managing team" was necessary, but proved difficult because no universally agreed upon definition exists. The term "self-managing team" has emerged in both the academic and popular press in recent years. For purposes of this study, the definition used was that of Cohen and Ledford's (1991): teams are "groups of interdependent individuals that can self-regulate their behavior on relatively whole tasks" (p. 3).

A better understanding of the required behaviors of the team leader is necessary in order to effectively prepare individuals for this role. Mohrman and Mohrman (1994) state that management team members frequently receive little team development opportunity because organizations assume they have already developed the needed skills through their management experience. Furthermore, these authors found that many organizations underestimate the amount of help team members and managers require to learn the new behaviors needed to operate in a team-based organization.

Wellins (1990) states, "Insufficient attention given to training is the single greatest barrier to a successful self-directed team installation." Likewise, Manz and Sims (1993) state that the most powerful ingredients for success with self-managing teams are training and learning opportunities to help managers through the transition to their new leadership roles. Therefore, a better understanding of specific behaviors required of team leaders, along with an increased understanding of the relationship these behaviors have to work team performance, will be helpful to organizational researchers and practitioners.

Some research exists concerning the needed leadership behaviors in teams. Manz & Sims (1990) identified the leadership behaviors of what they call a "SuperLeader." These authors stated that the challenge for the SuperLeader is to enable followers to discover the potential within themselves. Thus, the focus of leadership is on the relationship between the leader and follower. They identified seven leader behaviors: (1) modeling self-leadership, (2) encouraging self-set goals, (3) creating positive thought patterns, (4) developing self-leadership through reward and constructive reprimand, (5) promoting self-leadership culture, (6) facilitating a self-leadership culture, and (7) becoming an effective self-leader.

Similarly, Glaser (1991) identified six general "learning categories" of skill development for team leaders based upon his qualitative study of semi-autonomous work groups in a research library setting. The six categories for team leader learning that Glaser identified are: (1) learning a new leadership orientation, (2) learning to empower group members by transferring traditional leadership power to the team and developing the team's willingness to take responsibility, (3) learning to facilitate group self-management behaviors, such as team planning, goal setting, problem solving, conflict resolution, and decision making, (4) learning personal coping strategies, such as stress management and time management, (5) learning to facilitate the learning of others, and (6) learning how to learn from experience.

Moreover, Burress (1993) identified six categories of skills which team leaders need to strengthen or acquire in order to be effective leaders of self-managing teams: (1) communication—(listening to team members and sharing information in a clear and concise manner), (2) thinking skills—(attending to cues and analyzing problems effectively), (3) administration—(coordinating activities and paying attention to detail), (4) leadership—(encouraging responsibility and self-management), (5) interpersonal skills—(addressing personal problems and providing opportunities for personal and team growth), and (6) flexibility—(responding to the unexpected and taking advantage of opportunities). From this research, Burress developed the Self-managing Team (SMT) Leader Survey.

Each of the above-cited researchers has identified somewhat different team leader behaviors. In order to follow this stream of organizational research, this study will build on Burress' and Glaser's categories of team leader skills and behaviors. Specifically, this researcher was interested in determining whether Glaser's and Burress' categories were correct and if it was possible to relate these to real behaviors in teams. These questions formed the foundation for this study's research questions and hypothesis.

Research Questions

1. What are the necessary behaviors and skills of team leaders in leading self-managing teams?

2. Is there a relationship between team leadership skills and team performance?

Hypothesis

There is a positive relationship between the degree of team leader skills and team performance.

Null Hypothesis

Based on what is known about self-managing teams, the following null hypothesis will be tested:

There is no relationship between the degree of team leader skills and team performance.

SIGNIFICANCE OF THE STUDY

The results of this study will add to our understanding of the body of knowledge required for team leaders to succeed in team-based systems and will contribute empirical evidence by examining the relationship between team leadership and team performance.

A recent compilation of research on self-managing work teams found that nearly every major U.S. corporation is considering adopting this organizational design (Manz & Sims, 1993; Wellins, Byham & Wilson, 1991). In fact, Lawler (1996) states that his research on the Fortune 1000 U.S. corporations shows that teams are the fastest growing of the new work practices and are used by nearly every major U.S. corporation. The primary reasons cited for this shift are improved quality and productivity, greater flexibility in responding to customer needs, reduced operating costs, and improved worker satisfaction (Wellins, Wilson, Katz, Laughlin, & Day, 1990).

One of the most difficult issues in making the transition to teams is determining what to do with the first line of management (Peters, 1987). Yet, as several researchers have reported, this position is critical to the development of self-management (Kemp, Wall, Clegg & Cordery, 1983; Cummings, 1978; Ranney, 1986; Fotilas, 1981; Manz & Sims, 1987, 1989). When work teams are created, the number of managers needed can be reduced by more than 50% (Lawler, 1996). However, the elimination of management levels does not mean that teams won't need individuals who act as leaders and who assume responsibility for some management activities.

This study's results add to the body of knowledge of how teams work. The information will be useful to practitioners within organizations who are considering restructuring to a team-based design, by providing information critical to the training and development of team leaders for their new role. Additionally, the results will add to the theoretical and empirical work on the subject of leadership and performance in self-managing teams.

RESEARCH DESIGN

The quantitative research design of this study is shown in Figure 1. The nonexperimental quantitative design and data analysis process allowed for data collection from two survey instruments and for statistical analysis. This process formed the basis for examining the relationship between the independent variable, team leadership, and the dependent variable, team performance.

Independent Variable:	Dependent Variable:
Team Leadership	Team Performance
Dimensions:	Dimensions:
(Survey 1: SMT Leader Survey)	Production (Schedule and Quality)
• Communication	• Business Resources
• Thinking skills	Planning(BRP)
• Administration	• Business Planning and Control
• Leadership	System (BPCS)
• Interpersonal	
• Flexibility	
(Survey 2: Team Leader Survey)	
• Leadership	
• Empowerment	
• Self-management	
• Coping	
• Facilitating the learning of others	
• Facilitating own learning	

Note. This research design consisted of two phases: phase 1—instrument design and testing, phase 2—collection of performance data and correlational analysis.

Figure 1. Quantitative Research Design

Additional background research built a contextual framework for the study. The data analysis process used in this portion of the study was document analysis. Production records and staffing documents were reviewed to determine trends.

LIMITATIONS OF THE STUDY

Perhaps the primary limitation of this study is the lack of an experimental design with randomly selected subjects exposed to randomly assigned conditions. However, this is rarely achieved in an organizational setting. Hackman (1985) suggested that finding an organization that would allow the researchers to conduct such an experimental design would be such a rarity that the results gained could not be generalized to other organizations. Other limitations include the small sample size and that only one organization was included in the study; therefore, generalizability beyond the research site is difficult.

DEFINITIONS OF TERMS

Definitions of terms commonly used in the study are as follows:

Empowered Leadership: A new leadership orientation which involves learning to transfer traditional leadership power to the team, developing the team's willingness to take responsibility, and empowering team members (Glaser, 1991).

Self-management: Employee self-control or self-regulation is called self-management by Manz (1986). This perspective comes from Bandura's (1977) social learning theory which integrates cognitive evaluations with environmental contingencies as the determinants of human behavior. Thus, if employee behavior is based on internal control systems, then organizational control systems will only work to the degree that they influence the employee's self-control or self-regulating systems.

Self-managing teams: Groups of interdependent individuals that can self-regulate their behavior on relatively whole tasks (Cohen & Ledford, 1991).

Self-leader: Manz and Sims (1990) state that external leadership is replaced by self-leadership. The object of self-leadership, as well as self-management, is to replace reliance on external leadership with reliance on group leadership. To accomplish this goal, everyone must develop effective self-management skills.

CHAPTER 2

Literature Review

Several bodies of literature contribute to the understanding of how teams function, how to define effectiveness within team environments and the defining characteristics of team leaders. As shown in figure 2, this study concerns itself with the literature in the areas of organization design, self-managing teams, and adult learning concepts as they relate to team leadership roles and responsibilities. Self-managing teams occur in a general systems organization context:

- The focus on organization design was based on sociotechnical theory (Cummings, 1978.)

- The team leadership was based on Manz and Sims' (1987) theory of self-management, which is an application of social learning theory (Bandura, 1977).

- The focus on team performance was based on Cohen's (1993) indicators of work team effectiveness.

- The focus on adult learning theory was based on Mezirow's (1990) theory of perspective transformation. Although the intellectual roots are different, these theories overlapped as they were applied to self-managing teams, especially concerning the team leadership and team performance variables.

This chapter is divided into four major sections: (1) a summary of organization design literature, (2) a discussion of self-managing teams, including the effects of self-managing teams, team leadership with focus on Glaser's research and Burress' research, and team

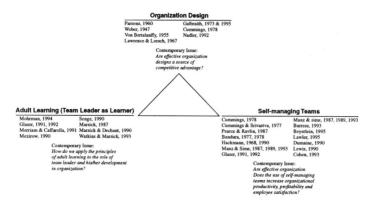

Figure 2. Integrative Framework for Literature Review

performance literature, (3) a review of adult-learning theory, and (4) a summary of the literature under review and discussion of the linkages among the various theories as they apply to self-managing teams.

ORGANIZATIONAL DESIGN

This section traces some strands of organization theory and design literature which led to the current interest in the team-based organization. This is important because self-managing teams occur in a general systems organization context.

The starting point came from Parsons' (1960) systems view of the organization subsystems and their imposition on Weber's (1947) bureaucratic form of organizations. Von Bertalanffy (1950, 1955), considered by some the father of general systems theory, conceptualized the organization as a system that interacts with its environment and which must adapt to changing environmental conditions. Later, contingency theorists found that an organization becomes more "organic" when it faces a dynamic and uncertain environment; organic systems are more capable of adapting to change (Burns & Stalker, 1961).

Galbraith's (1973) information-processing model of organization design provided a starting point for organizations to conceptualize how to adopt a more lateral framework that allows integration rather than relying on hierarchical integrating mechanisms. This early model consisted of a goal of "fit" among these five elements: tasks, structure, information and decision-making processes, people, and rewards. Galbraith (1995) revised his model to include strategy, resulting in these five elements: strategy, structure, information processes, rewards, and people.

The sociotechnical systems literature (Cummings, 1978) focused on the "fit" between the social system and technical system within the organization. This concept of a sociotechnical system arose from a consideration that any production-oriented organization involves both a technological system (equipment, task, and process design) and a social system (working relations). In routine settings, primarily manufacturing, this approach led to self-regulating teams, which have responsibility for a part of the conversion process. Cummings stated that "self-regulating work groups are a direct outgrowth of sociotechnical systems" (p. 45).

As more experience was gained with different design approaches, a growing number of companies in the 1980s began to integrate the sociotechnical, open systems, and new plant design concepts into an approach referred to as high-performance work systems (Lawler, 1978, 1986, 1987, 1992, 1995). This was a logical extension of the earlier frameworks.

The high-performance work systems approach to the design of human work organizations is an organizational architecture that brings together work, people, technology, and information. This approach optimizes the congruence or "fit" among them in order to produce high performance in terms of effective response to customer requirements and other environmental demands and opportunities (Nadler, Gerstein, & Shaw, 1992).

According to Galbraith (1995), organization design has been propelled to the top of the agenda for senior management. CEOs are getting involved because they see organization design decisions as priority and high leverage, and because they see effective organization design as a source of competitive advantage. Furthermore, Galbraith stated that solutions to many of today's business issues have their roots in organization design, and the choice of organization design ultimately depends on the organization's business strategy.

SELF-MANAGING WORK TEAMS

The concept of self-directed teams originated during the 1940s from Lewin's research at the Research Center for Group Dynamics and from the Tavistock Institute of Human Relations, where Emery and Trist conceptualized sociotechnical systems theory as an approach to designing organizations (Weisbord, 1987). The Tavistock group looked specifically at the interdependence between technology and people. "A concrete outcome of this theoretical perspective was the development of self-regulating work groups," according to Cummings (1978). Various authors have used the following group names: autonomous, self-managing, self-regulating, self-directed, or work teams. The common denominator across the initiatives is the goal of transferring control of the work process, over time, from the manager to members in the work unit.

Many researchers credit the work of Trist and his colleagues during the 1940s and 1950s with the origin and development of the self-managing or autonomous work team concept (Cummings & Srivastva, 1977). In fact, Trist became known as "the father of self-managing work teams" (SMWTs) because of his classic work in the British coal mines (Tubbs, 1994).

From the coal mining experiments, Tavistock researchers drew four major conclusions: (1) groups must be collectively responsible for a substantial but manageable piece of the business, (2) the work arrangement should facilitate social relationships that foster cooperation, (3) employees should have an opportunity to learn all of the jobs, and, (4) groups should have authority, materials and equipment necessary to perform their jobs, and feedback to evaluate their performance (Pearce & Ravlin, 1987). The theoretical outcomes of the Tavistock experiments, known as sociotechnical systems theory, provided a comprehensive framework for understanding and managing work. Simply stated, sociotechnical systems is an approach that attempts to jointly optimize both the social and technical aspects of the organization.

Cummings (1978) added to our understanding of work teams. He stated, "The design of self-regulating work groups depends on at least three conditions that enhance technically required cooperation and employees' capacity to control variances from goal attainment: task differentiation, boundary control, and task control" (p. 48). These conditions relate directly to a group's capacity for self-regulation.

Social learning theory (Bandura, 1977) is also deeply relevant to the self-managing work teams literature and to adult-learning concepts. In fact, Manz and Sims base their work on Bandura's theory. A central concept in social learning theory is the idea of reciprocal determinism

(Bandura, 1977, 1978), which argues that the person, behavior, and the external environment influence each other. Reciprocal determinism was initially conceived as persons and situations affecting each other, making them interdependent. Later Bandura expanded this concept to include interactions between behavior, cognitive and other personal factors, and environmental influences known as triadic reciprocity. Cohen (1993) identified the similar theoretical rationale between self-management and sociotechnical systems theory. Both theories emphasize self-regulation as the key mechanism, although self-management is applied to individuals while sociotechnical systems theory focuses on the group level. In other words, the strategies that are effective in increasing self-control at the individual level are applied to the group level in sociotechnical systems theory.

EFFECTS OF SELF-MANAGING TEAMS

Much contemporary writing on self-managing teams has concentrated on the economic results of the change to teams (Lawler, et al. 1995). Another body of literature, appearing primarily in the popular business press, has been predominantly practitioner-oriented and has described how self-managing teams increase organizational productivity, profitability, and employee satisfaction, in addition to explaining how corporations deal with the issues encountered during the transition to teams (Dumaine, 1990; Lewis, 1990). These transition issues include the following: (1) building trust between employees and management, (2) company management's fear of relinquishing control, (3) determining how to empower people to organize their work and make decisions, (4) providing training and support to team members, and (5) changing the compensation and performance appraisal systems (Dumaine, 1994). Clearly, the team leader would play a key role in leading teams through these transition issues.

TEAM LEADERSHIP

The role of the team leader has been the subject of increased interest and study. Effective leadership is critical to the success of teams, but the role of the team leader is not easy to master. Nadler (1995) described the challenge as follows:

> Corporations underestimate the shift in mindset and behavioral skills
> that team leaders need. Even the most capable managers have trouble

making the transition because all the command-and-control type things they were encouraged to do before are no longer appropriate. There's no reason to expect them to have any skill or sense of this (p. 93).

Manz and Sims (1987, 1989, 1993), who have done the most extensive study of the new role of the team leader, proposed an integrated perspective of team leader behaviors. These behaviors fall into seven categories: becoming a self-leader, modeling self-leadership, encouraging self-set goals, creating positive thought patterns, developing self-leadership through reward and constructive reprimand, promoting self-leadership through teamwork, and facilitating a self-leadership culture. These authors state that the challenge for the SuperLeader is to lead followers to discover the potential within themselves. Manz and Sims' (1987) observational study consisted of collecting qualitative data about the behaviors of external coordinators of self-managing work teams in a manufacturing plant. In this study, they found that external leaders encouraged and facilitated their employees to use these self-managing behavior strategies.

Bandura's social learning theory (1977) was the theoretical foundation for Manz and Sims' self-management theory (Manz, 1986). Bandura (1986) revised his theoretical framework from social learning theory to social cognitive theory. Sims and Lorenzi (1992) stated that self-management is both a behavioral and a cognitive issue. The way a team leader thinks and acquires information provides a critical link to the way he or she behaves. Sims and Lorenzi further stated that researchers are just beginning to understand how important cognition is as a part of effective management. These authors call the development of employee self-management the new leadership paradigm.

Manz and Sims (1993) described the role of the team leader as a facilitator. They state that one of the challenging and often overlooked aspects of implementing teams is the transition from supervisor to facilitator. Many times the emphasis is placed on the change the workers go through; however, Manz and Sims pointed out that the transition to self-managing teams is at least as challenging for middle level managers as for team members. The resistance of first level managers to the transition to self-managing teams has been cited in several studies, including Klein (1984).

Hackman (1990) concluded from his research that the role of the team leader or manager involves three kinds of activities: (1) creating favorable performance conditions for the team, (2) building and maintaining the team as a performing unit, and (3) coaching and helping the team in real time. Further, he suggests that team leaders might most appropriately focus their efforts on the creation of conditions that support effective team performance. In the popular business press, Caminiti (1995) defined the team leader job as "An unscientific blend of instinct, on-the-job learning, and patience" (p. 93). She states that the soft skills needed by team leaders are communication, conflict resolution, and coaching. In addition, she summed up the team leader role as confusing, hard to do, and hard to train for. As a result, Caminiti suggests that the best way to learn to be a team leader is to "learn by doing" (p. 100).

Glaser's Research

Glaser (1991), in his qualitative study of semi-autonomous work groups at the Yale University Library, identified six categories of learning for team leaders: (1) learning a new leadership orientation, (2) learning to empower group members, (3) learning to facilitate group self-management behaviors, (4) learning personal coping strategies, (5) learning to facilitate the learning of others, and (6) learning how to learn from experience.

Due to the importance of Glaser's research to the foundation of this study as the basis for the instrument development, a description of each of Glaser's learning categories is presented here. The first category, *learning a new leadership orientation*, involves several needs: clarifying the appropriate limits of authority, discovering the meaning and practical application of self-management concepts, learning to trust group members with responsibility normally reserved for the supervisor, and learning to trust oneself in the new, ambiguous role.

The second category, *learning to empower group members*, involves learning to transfer traditional leadership power to the team, developing the team's willingness to take responsibility, and empowering team members. The third category, *learning to facilitate group self-management behaviors*, involves teaching the group to manage themselves by planning its work, setting goals, monitoring its own performance, correcting that performance when it deviates from the expected standard, and rewarding the group for its performance. The fourth category, *learning personal coping strategies*, involves learning to manage stress and time constraints that accompany the conversion to self-management and a new team leader role.

The final two categories focus on the essential role that the learning process plays in changing from one work design to another. The fifth category, *learning to facilitate the learning of others*, involves the ability to train team members in the needed task skills, encouraging and supporting group members in training each other, facilitating individual and group learning of process or interpersonal skills such as giving and receiving feedback, facilitating group understanding of self-managing concepts, and helping the group to learn to think critically about work policies and processes.

The sixth category, *learning to learn from experience*, involves the team leader accepting responsibility for his/her own development, seeking formal and informal opportunities to learn at work, and learning from trial-and-error experience.

Glaser's research into the transition from a traditional work group to a self-managing team confirmed that this change is a major learning event. He states that the success of the team-based organization is dependent on the ability of the team members and the team leader to learn from their experiences and from each other. Moreover, he suggested that organizations and individuals approach the change as a continuing series of learning opportunities.

Burress' Research

Burress (1993) also conducted research on the role of team leaders. Burress' study of a manufacturing organization in the southwestern United States used six categories of critical skills which team leaders need to strengthen or acquire to be effective leaders of self-managing teams, specifically: (1) communication—listening to team members and sharing information clearly and concisely, (2) thinking skills—attending to cues (e.g., body language) and analyzing problems effectively, (3) administration—coordinating activities and paying attention to detail, (4) leadership—encouraging responsibility and self-management, (5) interpersonal skills—addressing personal problems and providing opportunities for personal and team growth, and (6) flexibility—responding to the unexpected and taking advantage of opportunities. Burress developed the SMT Leader Survey (Burress, 1994) consisting of 36 items that, in total, address the six categories of

Table 2.1: Comparison of Glaser's and Burress' Proposed Categories of Team Leader Behaviors

Glaser	Burress

Leadership
  Learning a new leadership orientation
	Leadership
	  Encouraging responsibility and self-management

Empowerment
  Learning to transfer traditional leadership power to the team, developing team's willingness to take responsibility, and empowering team members
	Communication
	  Listening to team members and sharing information in a clear and concise manner

Self-management
  Learning to facilitate team self-management behaviors, i.e., team planning, goal setting, problem solving, conflict resolution, decision making, etc.
	Administration
	  Coordinating activities and paying attention to detail

Personal Coping
  Learning personal coping strategies, i.e., stress and time management
	Thinking Skills
	  Attending to cues and analyzing problems effectively

Facilitate Learning of Others
  Learning to facilitate the learning of others
	Interpersonal Skills
	  Addressing personal problems and providing opportunities for personal and team growth

Facilitate own Learning
  Learning how to learn from experience
	Flexibility
	  Responding to the unexpected and taking advantage of opportunities

skills outlined above. Each item addresses a specific behavior or skill which, if developed, would contribute to self-managed team leader effectiveness.

In summary, although the identification of effective team leader behaviors has been proposed by Manz and Sims, Glaser, and Burress, a comprehensive and integrated framework still does not exist. A review of the similarities and differences proposed by these researchers is needed in order to add to our understanding of the specific behaviors of effective team leaders. Table 2.1 summarizes Glaser's and Burress' proposed categories of team leader behaviors.

Team Performance

The previous section covered the importance of team leadership. Equally important is the concept of team performance and how to measure it. While there is a general belief that teams make organizations more effective, few research efforts to measure this effectiveness have been described in the literature. The work that has been reported has focused primarily on manufacturing teams that can be assessed using operational measures such as productivity, efficiency, delivery time, defects, and amount of scrap (Beyerlein, 1995). Measuring the performance of teams in nonmanufacturing settings, such as professionals in science and engineering, may require more complex measures. In a review of the empirical literature on teams, Goodman, Devadas, and Hughson (1988) concluded that self-managing work teams have only a modest impact on performance.

According to Cohen (1993), the indicators of effectiveness for most work teams are based on their performance of three factors: controlling costs, increasing productivity, and increasing the quality of products or services. She further stated that these factors can be assessed by objective measurement or by evaluations by those who are knowledgeable about the team's work. Because most self-managing teams are created to improve performance, Cohen emphasized that they should, at minimum, have a positive impact on some facets of performance.

From a practical standpoint, organizations implementing self-managing teams should consider the intended outcome of such an intervention. Is the desired outcome improved quality, higher productivity, or improved employee satisfaction? Cohen (1993) suggested that if all three outcomes are intended, complex trade-offs may be necessary. She also pointed out that in current theory development, no integrated models describe different determinants of specific outcomes.

Lawler et al. (1995) found that Fortune 1000 companies perceived positive direct performance results from using self-managing teams. These companies perceived the strongest impact on outcomes such as quality of products and services, customer service, and productivity. However, Lawler's study did not find a positive correlation between self-managing teams and perceived increase in profitability and competitiveness.

Lawler et al. (1995) also examined the effect of employee involvement, which included self-managing teams, and total quality management practices on companies' financial performance. While the analysis focused on the company, not the team, this study found that the use of employee involvement and total quality management practices was significantly related to six measures of corporate performance: total factor productivity, sales per employee, return on sales, return on assets, return on investment, and return on equity. Lawler concluded: "The finding of a significant relationship suggests that there may be a causal relationship between the adoption of management practices and firm performance." (p. 90).

Clearly, the problems of measuring team performance are complex. Often the existing performance measurement systems in place are not aligned with new initiatives, such as self-managing teams. In these cases, the measurement systems do not adequately reflect the impact on efficiency and effectiveness of new initiatives (Beyerlein, 1995). If there are problems with the performance measurement system, it is difficult, if not impossible, to evaluate the value of self-managing teams.

Adult Learning

Adult learning is important because it relates directly to team leadership and team performance. As mentioned earlier, Bandura's concept of self-efficacy is an important foundation for thinking of the team leader as an adult learner. It is important to consider how this learning might occur and the linkages among adult learning, team leadership, and team performance. Adult learning concepts, as they relate to team leadership roles and responsibilities, are reviewed in this section.

Organizational changes leading to self-managing work teams typically involve flattening the organization by removing management layers, thus shifting traditional management duties to the teams. The team leader's role becomes one of coaching team members to assume these former management duties and become self-managing. Although many companies are experimenting with this new work design, little research exists examining the required behaviors of team leaders as they are transitioned to work within this new environment. Yet, learning these new behaviors may be critical to the team leaders' success in their new role.

Learning is required for organizations to generate and implement new approaches and designs, and to continuously improve and evolve their techniques (Watkins & Marsick, 1993). Organizational members must also learn, individually and collectively, how to operate differently within organizations. Organizational learning occurs in many ways, including formal education, informal experience-based learning, collective visioning and planning processes. During fundamental organizational transitions, employees must individually and collectively learn and develop new approaches and new ways of understanding their organization and performing within it (Mohrman, 1994).

During transitions, a major challenge is to help organizational members learn to be effective in the new organization, and to establish a learning environment to support ongoing change. This requires a willingness to adopt new roles, reflect on behavior and performance, introduce behavioral changes, and continually assess and improve (Mohrman, 1994).

It is clear that learning is critical to the team leaders' success as they transition to their new role. However, learning in adulthood is more than adding to what one already knows, and certainly occurs outside the traditional classroom. A review of adult-learning theory offered insights regarding creating learning environments.

Perhaps Merriam and Caffarella (1991) offered the most comprehensive review of adult-learning theory. These authors organized the theory in three categories: (1) those that focus on adult characteristics (e.g., Knowles, 1980; Cross, 1979), (2) those that emphasize an adult's life situation (e.g., McClusky, 1963; Knox, 1977, and Jarvis, 1987), and (3) those that center on changes in consciousness (e.g., Mezirow, 1990; Freire, 1970). They summarized these categories as the adult, the context, and the learning process.

Merriam and Caffarella (1991) contend that more than the other theories cited above, Mezirow's theory deals most directly with learning in adulthood. The defining characteristic of adult learning is the change in perspective or consciousness, according to Mezirow's and Freire's theories. Merriam and Caffarella state that for Mezirow and Freire, learning in adulthood is a transformative process rather than an additive one. New learning transforms existing knowledge into a new perspective. Learning requires the ability for critical reflection, a uniquely adult skill. Both theorists accounted for adult characteristics and the sociocultural context. However, the two differ in the notion of being emancipated through this learning process. For Freire, being emancipated requires political action aimed at changing society, while Mezirow emphasized personal psychological change. Of all the theories, Mezirow's on perspective transformation was the most inclusive of context, learner, and process (Merriam & Caffarella, 1991).

Mezirow (1990) defined perspective transformation as follows:

Perspective transformation is the process of becoming critically aware of how and why our presuppositions have come to constrain the way we perceive, understand, and feel about our world; of reformulating these assumptions to permit a more inclusive, discriminating, permeable, and integrative perspective, and of making decisions or otherwise acting upon these new understandings. More inclusive, discriminating, permeable, and integrative perspectives are superior perspectives that adults choose if they can because they are motivated to better understand the meaning of their experience (p. 14).

Furthermore, Mezirow (1990) stated that learning is a four-stage process: (1) extending meaning schemes, (2) creating new meaning schemes, (3) altering old meaning schemes, and (4) enabling perspective transformation. The process of perspective transformation begins with a "disorienting dilemma" to which one's old response patterns are no longer appropriate or effective. This dilemma causes a self-examination of one's assumptions and beliefs. Based on this four-stage process, Mezirow believes that adults learn by either changing their perspective based on current knowledge and experiences or based on obtaining new information. He further stated that adults learn by "making meaning" of their experiences, and that what happens to an individual is not as important as how the person interprets the events and makes meaning from them.

The concept of a "disorienting dilemma" may very well apply to team leaders as they transition from a traditional supervisory role to a leader of a self-managing team. Glaser (1991) found that this transition involves giving up the familiar image of the traditional boss, and learning a completely new orientation to leadership. Surely, one's old patterns of response would not be effective. This situation would most likely precipitate a self-examination and assessment of one's assumptions and beliefs about the workplace. Glaser found that considerable time and effort is required to learn and adapt to a self-managing environment.

Applying Mezirow's thinking to creating a learning culture in a self-directed team environment would lead to a logical conclusion that emphasis should be placed on developing experiences that build upon an individual's past experiences, as well as developing a process for helping individuals create dialogue with others having a similar experience. Mezirow referred to this as communicative learning, i.e., better understanding of self and others through dialogue. Senge (1990) and Schein (1993) also stressed the need for dialogue as a reflective learning process, which focuses on the quality of conversation and capability for collective thinking. Senge pointed out the Greek roots for dialogue, "dia" and "logos," suggest "meaning flowing through," a much deeper type of communication than traditional discussion. Similarly, Glaser (1992) suggested using dialogue sessions with team leaders by organizing informal get-togethers where they would share and reflect on their experiences and attempt to learn more from their own experiences. He adds that through dialogue and reflection, a leader's orientation can be modified gradually.

It is clear that team leaders have substantial new learning to acquire if they are to be successful in their new role and if organizations are to realize the potential of self-managing teams. Marsick and Dechant (1990) called for the creation of complete learning organizations where:

> Learning is integrated into the ongoing daily operations and worklife of employees so that they can continuously improve their performance, and the organization can capture the benefits of their learning in the form of new knowledge, work procedures, systems, thinking or behaviors . . . (p. 2).

In summary, the self-managing team concept offers a viable beginning to the development of the learning organization. Certainly the concepts of adult learning provide critical insights into the essential process of learning in the workplace.

SUMMARY

The theory and research on organization design, self-managing teams, and adult learning have pursued different avenues to efforts directed toward the construct of organizational effectiveness. Factors identified concerning how organizational design, self-managing teams, and adult-learning come together to positively influence organizations are not well developed.

Theories on organizational design have focused on the design of human work organizations. In recent years, the attention paid to design has increased as organizations attempt to use effective organizational design to improve their competitive advantage.

Theories on self-managing teams have focused on the ability of groups to self-manage or self-regulate their work behavior. Additionally, research has attempted to determine the characteristics of effective team leaders, as well as appropriate measures of team performance.

Theories on adult learning have focused on identifying principles and conditions that enable adults to learn most effectively. These principles, when applied to the workplace, help to define how practitioners could best use adult-learning techniques to design learning experiences at work.

The research questions developed for this study reflect current issues concerning the learning of team leaders and the relationship between team leader skills and the performance of the work team. These questions demonstrate an interest in understanding how organizations can best prepare team leaders for their roles and determine how team leadership is related to team performance.

CHAPTER 3
Methodology

This research project employed a nonexperimental quantitative research design. As previously shown in figure 1, this study examined the relationship between the variables of team leadership and team performance. Pearson correlation and Spearman rank correlation were used to determine the relationship of the independent variable, team leadership, to the dependent variable, team performance. Because correlation coefficients "are best used to measure the *degree* of relationship between two variables and to explore *possible* causal factors that can later be tested in an experimental design" (Borg & Gall, 1989, p. 576), this study proposed no causal inferences between these factors, but was intended to identify only *potential* relationships which may be tested by future research.

BACKGROUND OF THE ORGANIZATION

This research was conducted in a manufacturing division of a Fortune 100 pharmaceutical company located in the northeastern United States. The company is a 1991 joint-venture between two Fortune 100 companies, one a major pharmaceutical company and the other a major chemical company. The company is midsize and has a manufacturing division of approximately 700 employees. The president of the manufacturing division decided to restructure into teams in 1993 in order to increase the organization's competitiveness in a rapidly changing industry. The research site, a manufacturing facility, was running two shifts and produced various generic drugs. The environment was clean, modern, well-lighted, and highly automated. Plant employees wore white uniforms, hair covers, and safety glasses in designated areas. Typically, employees had worked for the company for several years (either the joint-venture company or the previous parent company).

Research Methodology

This research was conducted in two phases. Phase 1 consisted of instrument development and testing through factor analysis; phase 2 dealt with collection of team leadership, team performance measures and correlational analysis. Team leadership behaviors were assessed through the administration of two surveys. Correlation analysis was used to determine the relationship of the independent variable (team leadership) to the dependent variable (team performance). This section will describe the study's procedures, sample selection, and data gathering.

Selection of Research Site

At a minimum, one organizational site with multiple production teams was needed for the study. Although each site is unique, one was identified that typified self-managing organizations, as described in the literature (Manz & Sims, 1993). Criteria for site selection included:

1. The length of time self-managing teams had been operational was considered. The facility must have been structured into self-managing teams for at least 12 months. Most organizations take 12 months to launch teams after the redesign. Transition periods can be prolonged due to the necessary changes in tasks, structure, information and decision-making processes, reward systems, and people systems (Galbraith, 1973). The assumption was that a 12-month period provides adequate time for most early transition and implementation changes to occur.

2. In terms of structural changes, the role of supervisor must have been eliminated and the position of team leader created. These team leaders reported to functional managers of the site leadership team, which included the plant manager. It should be noted that the structural changes at the site involved eliminating one layer of middle management.

3. The teams had to meet the definition of self-managing as specified in this study, i.e., members had day-to-day

responsibility for managing themselves and their work. As expected in this type of transition, not all teams were progressing at the same pace toward self-management.

4. Adequate field access to team leaders, team members, and top management was required.

The research site had 11 self-managing teams, each with a separate team leader. In addition, the site leadership team included the plant manager and four functional managers. In some cases, the team leader positions were filled by former line supervisors; in other cases, workers were promoted into the positions. All team leaders had received four days of introductory team leader training prior to implementation and approximately 30 hours of team training after team implementation. The training methods employed were traditional classroom training based on lecture, as well as occasional role plays, exercises, video segments, and class discussion.

The first four days of classroom training were custom designed by the internal corporate training department and covered such topics as defining teams vs. work groups, managing change, developmental stages of teams, defining roles of team leaders and team members, transition issues, behavior management of individuals vs. teams, conflict resolution, and coaching and counseling. The following 30 hours of team training focused on skills for facilitating team development. This training presented a model of team development based upon building trust, establishing goals, defining roles, determining procedures, and improving relationships. (Although all original team leaders participated in the initial training, it should be noted that during the course of the research, one team leader was replaced by an individual who had not received the team leader training.)

Sample Selection

Participants were team members or team leaders of intact self-managing teams within one division of the company. A team was defined as "a group of interdependent individuals that can self-regulate their behavior on relatively whole tasks" (Cohen and Ledford, 1991, p. 3). Additionally, each team consisted of individuals who reported to one team leader. This allowed aggregation of data to the group level.

The teams included in this study were those involved in the daily operations of the manufacturing plant: four manufacturing teams, three quality teams, and four support teams (i.e., planning and technical services, human resources, and building services). Although this was a manufacturing environment, it was not a typical or traditional manufacturing setting, as can be noted from the descriptive statistics, especially the educational levels. Table 3.1 provides descriptive statistics for the total population in phase 1 of the study. The population was 53% male, 47% female, with 60% Caucasian and 40% minority. The average age was 40, and 71% had been members of their team for 12 months. The population was highly educated, with 76% reporting educational levels greater than a high school level. The total population (N=140) was used for the phase 1 factor analysis. Because phase 1 concerned itself with defining team leader behaviors through the testing of two instruments, both team leaders and team members were included in this phase of the study. Thus, 11 team leaders and 129 team members participated in phase 1.

However, in phase 2, the data from the subset of that population were used for the correlational analysis with performance data. This subset included only team members (*n*=118), and deleted two teams without performance data, thus leaving nine teams for further analysis. Appendix A provides demographic data on the subjects included in phase 2 of the study.

Table 3.1: Description of Total Sample (*N*=140)

Respondents	Mode	Range	Other Comments
Age	40-49 yrs. (28.6%)	Less than 20 to more than 60	
Ethnic	60% White		14% Asian 13.1% Black 7.0% Other 6% Hispanic .8% No answer
Seniority on this Team	71% = 12 Months	Less than 1 month to 12 months	Mean = 10 mo's.
Education	28.7% Some college	High school to masters degree	76% College educated
Sex	53% Male		47% Female

DATA GATHERING

Several data collection methods were used to measure the variables involved in the study. The methods are described and categorized in the following sections.

Phase 1: Instrumentation

Two instruments were used as data collection tools. Although a review of literature on team leadership provided no previously validated instrument on team leadership, discussion with professionals in the field yielded an instrument under development by Burress. This section reviews the development of Burress' instrument.

Development of the Self-Managing Team (SMT) Leader Survey

The Self Managing Team (SMT) Leader Survey is a behaviorally focused instrument measuring 36 skills on six dimensions that Burress (1993) found most important to effective team leadership. This survey was developed through a research study that was conducted in several phases over a two-year period. Phase 1 consisted of a job analysis of team leaders in a manufacturing setting. This job analysis identified critical SMT leader skills. Phase 2 consisted of the development of the test version of the SMT. Phase 3 consisted of data analysis of the test version. The test version of the SMT was a 50-item questionnaire that integrated the knowledge, skills, and abilities statements from the phase 1 job analysis. Individuals from 44 companies and 21 states and Canada completed the test version of the survey, with a total of 97 participants. Burress found that the team leader behaviors identified in the phase 1 job analysis and the SMT clearly reflected what were considered in the literature to be important components of team leadership.

The responses to the test version of the SMT were statistically analyzed by Burress. Due to the small N, Burress was unable to perform factor analysis of the data. Thus, she had experts sort the 50 items into eight categories of an instrument developed by Personnel Decisions, Inc. This instrument, Profiler Plus, served as a model defining these broad areas of leadership. Inter-item reliability was used and a reliability coefficient of .70 for the dimension was required for inclusion in further analysis.

The resulting reliability coefficients were as follows: administration .85; leadership .84; communication .80; cognitive (thinking skills) .76; interpersonal skills .72; motivation .67; personal adaptability .48; and technical knowledge .36. Consequently, the dependent variables of motivation, personal adaptability, and technical knowledge were dropped from further analysis. The remaining categories formed the basis of the current SMT Leader Survey: communication, thinking skills, administration, leadership, interpersonal skills, and flexibility (although it is unclear why the personal adaptability category was renamed "flexibility" and included again).

Additional testing of the instrument was concluded in 1995. Analysis of reliability of the instrument revealed high internal reliability, indicating that the instrument could be expected to produce similar results under similar circumstances. Analysis of the internal reliability of each subscale indicated high reliability for each subscale. The Cronbach alpha, a type of internal consistency reliability for items with scaled responses, ranged from .81 to .89 for individual scales.

Development of the Team Leader Survey (TLS)

The second survey used in this study was the Team Leader Survey (TLS). After determining the six dimensions to be studied, based upon Glaser's (1991) study results, a search was made for an instrument to measure these six aspects of team leader behavior. Instruments were found that measured some aspects (such as Burress' SMT), but it was not possible to find one that measured all six dimensions. Interest in team leader behaviors is relatively new and research on this topic is recent. For these reasons, the development of the Team Leader Survey (TLS) was undertaken.

A preliminary list of 31 questions was developed and grouped into six categories, identified by Glaser's research. The items were written in questionnaire format and reviewed by technical and subject matter experts. Their feedback resulted in the modification of several items to provide greater clarity. Additionally, the items were reviewed by two members of management at the research site. No revisions resulted from this review.

The 31-item version was then administered to 142 members of the pharmaceutical manufacturing organization (with 140 usable instruments obtained). Appendix D contains the TLS instrument. A Varimax factor analysis was completed and the factor loadings reviewed. As a result, six items were discarded because the coefficients were less than .60. Items with coefficients less than .60 were determined to be weak questions and were eliminated. Two interrelated but distinct scales resulted from the factor analysis of the 25-item instrument. Reliability and validity of this instrument are addressed later in this chapter. The study design contributed to a participation rate of 77% (142 employees out of 185 possible participated). Because the survey questionnaires were administered in team meetings during normal working hours, all members present completed the surveys.

Phase 2: Team Performance Data Collection

Performance measures of the teams were collected, based upon adherence to schedule and quality. Each team's performance was measured according to percentage attainment of goal. This study employed a performance measure that allowed a comparison of productivity across all teams in the study. Because this study was conducted in the pharmaceutical industry, measures of performance common to that industry were selected. Typically, pharmaceutical manufacturing includes a performance measure called business resources planning (BRP). This business process is used to maintain control of manufacturing schedules and inventory. BRP includes: the production plan, the master production schedule, schedule performance, inventory accuracy, bill of material accuracy, supplier performance, and cycle-time performance.

The standardized procedures for being certified as a "Class A" BRP facility were applied at this facility, which had attained "Class A" status. This status involves testing, validation, and certification by a recognized external consulting firm on an annual basis. In addition, the internal requirements for a site to receive "Class A" status required 13 consecutive weeks of adherence to BRP performance metrics. This research site had attained "Class A" status at the time of this study.

Additionally, employees of this facility collected local performance measures through a business planning and control system (BPCS), a commercially available software system. The measures in this system were: number of batches manufactured and packaged, material handling sampling and release, and quality control of incoming material and finished product.

The research site used both systems, BRP and BPCS, as a fully integrated system which tracks business information throughout the company. This provided extensive performance data used in this study.

Measures were collected at two points in time. Time 1 was the week of March 3, 1995, when the researcher was on-site administering the team leader surveys. This coincided with the site completion of its first year in self-managing teams. Time 2 was the week of April 28, nearly two months later. It is noteworthy that product cycle time was 15 days and, therefore, did not influence the data collection time periods. The measurements taken at time 2 ensured that the data collected had not been affected by the researcher's presence on-site at time 1.

DATA ANALYSIS

This section describes the phase 1 factor analysis and the phase 2 correlational analysis.

Phase One: Factor Analysis

A factor analysis is appropriate for investigating a dataset to determine the underlying patterns of intercorrelations among variables (Fields, 1984). This technique is used with both survey instruments in order to study the structure of team leadership dimensions and to determine how the common variance of the responses are distributed across a number of dimensions.

Factor analysis is a statistical method of identifying distinct factors or scales, i.e., items that group together within an inventory or questionnaire. The Team Leader Survey (TLS) has two factors. What follows is a description of how these factors were obtained.

A Varimax analysis of the TLS data identified two factors. Six questions were deleted from the instrument because their coefficients were less than .60. Of the remaining 25 items, 18 items clustered in factor 1 and 7 items clustered in factor 2. Each of the items loaded at .60 and higher. The total variance accounted for in these two factors was 62.26%, with factor 1's proportion at 40.01% and factor 2's proportion at 22.25%.

The statements in each factor were analyzed to see how they related to the original six categories from which they were derived. Factor 1 related to the broad area of leadership, empowerment, self-management, facilitating the learning of others, and personal coping. Factor 2 contained all the items from the learning how to learn category and one item from the personal coping category, with all items resulting in negative factor loadings. Table 3.2 provides the factor loadings of items in the TLS.

Table 3.2: Factor Loadings for TLS (*N*=140)

Item	F1	F2
Clearly defining role relationships	.72	-.20
Helping team members take responsibility for team's work	.68	-.18
Helping team members learn to work together better as a team	.72	-.32
Helping team members learn to work together better interpersonally	.75	-.34
Helping team members learn to plan their activities	.78	-.29
Helping team members learn how to implement group tasks	.72	-.40
Helping team members learn how to communicate better	.66	-.33
Helping team members learn how to solve problems as a group	.75	-.37
Helping team members learn how to make decisions as a group	.74	-.33
Helping team members learn how to resolve own conflicts	.79	-.14
Helping team members learn how to check and correct own work	.71	-.32
Helping team members learn how to reinforce effective team behaviors	.70	-.41
Helping team members learn how to discipline themselves	.67	-.39
Helping team members learn how to get the job skills needed	.75	-.30
Helping team members learn how to get self-managing skills	.66	-.42
Helping team members understand what it means to be a self-managing team	.63	-.44
Learning to manage difficult people assertively	.62	-.33

Table 3.2 (continued)

Item	F1	F2
Developing and using new team process facilitation skills	.64	-.49
Developing and using new systems and procedures to improve own technical expertise	.55	-.59
Using what was learned from formal training experiences	.47	-.64
Using informal learnings from colleagues	.34	-.69
Using learnings from other team members	.48	-.64
Using learnings from own reading	.32	-.67
Using learnings from mentors	.12	-.90
Using learnings from trial and error experiences	.20	-.73

Correlation of TLS Factors

To determine whether the two factors were correlated and could be treated as one independent variable, Pearson Product Moment correlations were computed for each factor with the total TLS and for each factor to the other.

Table 3.3 presents the correlation coefficient for each factor of TLS. Correlations were significant for all factors ($p<.05$).

Table 3.3: Correlation Coefficients for TLS Factors

	Total	Factor 1
Factor 1: Leadership	.98	
Factor 2: Learning	.74	.62

Means and Standard Deviations

Table 3.4 presents the mean score and standard deviations for each factor and total of TLS.

The factors were significantly correlated with each other and to the total TLS. The results showed the factors were strongly interrelated and yet distinguishable. To a lesser degree, content and construct validity

Table 3.4: Mean Score and Standard Deviation for Factors of TLS

Scale	Mean	SD	N
Total	107.62	11.67	9
Factor 1: Leadership	61.57	7.90	9
Factor 2: Learning	25.43	2.35	9

have been demonstrated, in that expert judgments were used to develop and refine the measures. Also, factor analysis of the data obtained showed that the constructs of leadership and learning are distinct, although the proposed six dimensions were not found.

Reliability

The reliability of the two instruments was reviewed. First, concerning the SMT leader survey, five of the six dimensions with a reliability coefficient of .70 or greater were retained by Burress in the final version of the survey. One dimension had coefficient data originally missing, i.e., the flexibility dimension. Reliability analyses for the TLS were obtained by using Cronbach's alpha, generally the most appropriate type of reliability for questionnaires and survey research in which there is a range of possible answers for each item (McMillan & Schumacher, 1989).

The reliability coefficients for the entire TLS instrument, as well as for each factor, were quite high indicating strong internal consistency. The total reliability coefficient for all TLS items was .97. Likewise, the SMT reliability coefficient for all items was .95. For training and development purposes, a coefficient of .70 is considered acceptable (Sashkin & Glaser, 1990). Appendix C contains the reliability data.

Internal and External Validity

Validity describes the extent to which an instrument measures what it is supposed to measure. Concerning the instrumentation, there are several ways to demonstrate an instrument's validity: construct validity, content validity, concurrent validity, and predictive validity. The SMT Leader Survey proved content validity through a job analysis of team leaders in a manufacturing setting. This job analysis identified critical SMT leader skills.

The TLS demonstrated content validity based on an extensive review of current research and literature; it was solidly grounded in current theory regarding self-managing teams. Concurrent validity was tested between the TLS and the SMT, even though Burress' SMT was not fully validated. In this study, 140 respondents completed both instruments. Correlations between the two instruments were strong and significant. The total TLS and SMT correlation coefficient was .80 ($p<.01$) by the original six dimensions of each survey.

Construct validity was tested by factor analyses, which failed to validate six factors for either instrument. The original six dimensions with 31 items of the TLS sorted into two primary factors which accounted for 59% of the variance. After six items were deleted from the survey, the two factors accounted for 62% of the variance. Similarly, the original six dimensions of the SMT sorted into two primary factors which accounted for 49% of the variance. Predictive validity was not tested in this study.

PHASE TWO: DATA ANALYSIS

The correlation method was selected to allow analysis of six dimensions of team leadership from each survey, and to provide information concerning the degree of relationship between the independent variable, team leadership, and the dependent variable, team performance.

The researcher obtained two performance scores (percentage attainment of goal) for each team, one from BRP metrics and one from BPCS metrics, for each time period. These two pairs of scores were then used to calculate correlation coefficients for the teams. The Pearson correlation is appropriately applied when both variables use continuous scales. Also, the Spearman rank correlation was used as the data was rank ordered. According to McMillan and Schumacher (1989) the correlational research method is used for two main purposes: (1) relationship studies and (2) prediction studies. The primary limitation to using the correlation method is that correlation does not imply causation. The reason for this is that a relationship may be strong, but there is no way to know from a correlation whether X causes Y or Y causes X. Although correlation does not determine causality, the results can be used to test whether relationships exist between the variables

Background Data

An element of background research was added in order to explore the environment in which the quantitative data collection occurred.

Understanding the organizational setting and context added to the richness of this study. Document analysis was used during the phase 2 data collection. It consisted of reviewing three years of production records, as well as 30 months of staffing records. These documents were important to the organization and sensitized the researcher to the site's production environment. A spreadsheet was developed based upon this data which allowed assessment of the upward trends of both production volume and staffing levels. A productivity ratio was developed from the spreadsheet analysis.

Ethical Considerations

Organizational members participating in this research were informed of all aspects of the study; participation was voluntary. The researcher promised the participants confidentiality of individual scores. The organization involved was, however, identified with prior permission.

All participants were given the opportunity to ask questions about the study. The study results were reviewed with the team leaders, the managers, plant manager, and the president of the manufacturing division.

SUMMARY

The design and methodology outlined in this chapter were selected to reflect the nature of the area under study and to reveal the relationship between team leadership and team performance. The findings of these methods are discussed in chapter 4.

Results

This chapter examines descriptive data and results of the data analyses. The major intent of the study was to examine the relationship between team leadership and team performance. To accomplish this aim, it was necessary to develop an instrument to assess team leadership. Such an instrument would have to identify and assess team leader skills and behavior.

The first section of this chapter presents the phase 1 results of the factor analysis of both survey instruments, the Team Leader Survey (TLS) and the SMT Leader Survey. The second section presents the phase two results of the correlation analysis, which explored the relationship between team leadership and team performance. The third section presents the test results on the differences between high- and low-performing teams in terms of team leadership. The fourth section presents the results of the background research, which explored the environment in which the teams were working. The fifth section presents an overview of the research results and ends with a recapitulation of the main findings.

The first research question was stated as follows: What are the necessary behaviors and skills of team leaders in leading self-managing teams? This question was examined using two separate instruments to assess these skills, the Team Leader Survey (TLS) and the SMT Survey Leader. A factor analysis of each instrument was performed; the results are described in this section.

PHASE 1: FACTOR ANALYSES

Factor Analysis of the Team Leader Survey (TLS—Kraft)

Several factor analyses of the team leadership dimensions were conducted to test Glaser's (1991) proposed six dimensions of team leadership. The six dimensions were: leadership, empowerment, self-management, personal coping skills, facilitating the learning of others, and facilitating one's own learning (learning how to learn). Principal components analysis with Varimax rotation was performed on 31 items from the Team Leader Survey (TLS). Principal components extraction was used to estimate the number of factors. In this dataset 140 cases were analyzed.

Several iterations resulted in two factors extracted from the instrument. Six items proved unstable with less than .60 coefficient on the Varimax and were deleted from the final solution. The deleted items were: #2. Cooperates effectively with leaders and members of other teams, #15. Helps team members learn to select new colleagues, #16. Helps team members learn to adjust to changes in the team's organization, #20. Helps team members learn to think for themselves, #21. Team leader uses time management techniques, and, #22. Team leader uses stress management techniques.

Communality values, as seen in table 4.1, tended to be medium to high, with a range of .49 to .82.

Eigenvalues for the two factors were factor 1 = 10.00 (40.01% of the variance), and factor 2 = 5.56 (22.25% of the variance). The two factors accounted for 62.26% of the total variance in this sample. The results of the Varimax factor analysis are shown in table 4.2.

Factor 1, the largest in number of items and amount of variance accounted for, contains many task- and performance-oriented behaviors which generally focus on "helping the team members learn." This factor contains items from five of the six dimensions, specifically: leadership, empowerment, self-management, facilitating the learning of others, and personal coping. Factor 1 is identified as a general leadership orientation toward empowering others.

Factor 2 accounts for a much smaller percentage of the variance. These items focus on the learning of the team leader himself or herself. This factor includes all six items in the dimension of learning how to learn and one item from the personal coping dimension, with all items

Table 4.1: Communality Values of TLS

Item	Communality
Clearly defining role relationships	.55
Helping team members take responsibility for team's work	.50
Helping team members learn to work together better as a team	.62
Helping team members learn to work together better interpersonally	.68
Helping team members learn to plan their activities	.69
Helping team members learn how to implement group tasks	.68
Helping team members learn how to communicate better	.54
Helping team members learn how to solve problems as a group	.69
Helping team members learn how to make decisions as a group	.66
Helping team members learn how to resolve own conflicts	.64
Helping team members learn how to check and correct own work	.61
Helping team members learn how to reinforce effective team behaviors	.65
Helping team members learn how to discipline themselves	.60
Helping team members learn how to get the job skills needed	.65
Helping team members learn how to get self-managing skills	.60
Helping team members understand what it means to be a self-managing team	.60
Learning to manage difficult people assertively	.49
Developing and using new systems and procedures to improve my own technical expertise	.65
Developing and using new team process facilitation skills	.65
Using what was learned from formal training experiences	.63
Using informal learnings from colleagues	.60
Using learnings from other team members	.64
Using learnings from own reading	.55
Using learnings from mentors	.82
Using learnings from trial and error experiences	.58

Table 4.2: Varimax Factor Analysis of TLS

Item	Loading	
	F1	F2
Clearly defining role relationships	.72	-.20
Helping team members take responsibility for team's work	.68	-.18
Helping team members learn to work together better as a team	.72	-.32
Helping team members learn to work together better interpersonally	.75	-.34
Helping team members plan learn to plan their activities	.78	-.29
Helping team members learn how to implement group tasks effectively	.72	-.40
Helping team members learn how to communicate better	.66	-.33
Helping team members learn how to solve problems as a group	.75	-.37
Helping team members learn how to make decisions as a group	.74	-.33
Helping team members learn how to resolve own conflicts	.79	-.14
Helping team members learn how to check and correct own work	.71	-.32
Helping team members learn how to reinforce effective team behaviors	.70	-.41
Helping team members learn how to discipline themselves	.67	-.39
Helping team members learn how to get the job skills needed	.75	-.30
Helping team members learn how to get the self-managing skills needed	.66	-.42
Helping team members understand what it means to be a self-managing team	.63	.44
Learning to manage difficult people assertively	.62	-.33
Developing and using new team process facilitation skills	.64	-.49
Developing and using new systems and procedures to improve my own technical expertise	.55	-.59
Using learnings from formal training experiences	.47	-.64
Using informal learning from colleagues	.34	-.69
Using learnings from other team members	.48	-.64
Using learnings from reading on my own	.32	-.67
Using learnings from mentors	.12	-.90
Using learnings from trial and error experiences	.20	-.73

resulting in negative factor loadings. These items generally focus on "using what I learn." Factor 2 is identified as a general learning category focused on the team leader's learning strategies.

FACTOR ANALYSIS SMT LEADER SURVEY

This researcher provided the SMT survey author (Burress) raw data from this study, which was then combined with data from Burress' study of a large U.S. customer service organization. Both datasets were combined to create a larger pool of participants used by Burress in the factor analysis of the SMT Leader Survey. Combining the data yielded a total N of 328 for the factor analysis. The 328 cases analyzed provided a ratio of nine cases per variable, which is considered good (Tabachnick & Fidell, 1989.) The Kaiser-Meyer-Olkin Measure of sampling adequacy was .97, which is greater than the .6 required for a good factor analysis.

Principal components analysis with Varimax rotation was performed on 32 items from the SMT Leader Survey. Principal components extraction was used to estimate the number of factors. Several iterations resulted in three factors extracted for the instrument. Four items proved unstable and were deleted from the final solution. Deleted were the following items: #3. Obtain resources for team members, #8. Solve team problems on my own, #9. Establish priorities for the team, and #13. Keep information to myself. Communality values tended to be high on the remaining items, ranging from .47 to .90.

Eigenvalues for the three factors were: factor 1 = 16.87 (52.7% of the variance), factor 2 = 5.17% (16.1% of the variance), and factor 3 = 1.25 (3.9%) of the variance. These three factors accounted for 72.7% of the total variance in this sample. Items in factor 1 contained many task- and performance-associated behaviors, similar to the "initiation of structure" from the Ohio State University studies on leadership behavior (Hemphill, 1950). Factor 2 items were related to "consideration of employees" and addressed interpersonal interaction of the team leader with his/her team. Factor 3 consisted of a small group of negatively scored items from the instrument. These three factors are also similar to those identified by Bales (1958). The first two of Bales' dimensions involved behavior centered on task accomplishment and behavior that was directed toward interpersonal relations, which he labeled "socio-emotional relationship" behavior. Bales' third factor consisted of negative, self-centered behavior items. Internal consistency reliability computed for the factors was: factor 1 = .98, factor 2 = .52, and factor 3 = .86. The Rotated Factor Matrix Solution with the items and their correlation with each of the respective factors is shown in table 4.3. Burress provided to this researcher the following data which represents the combined dataset (N=328).

As noted earlier in describing the selection and testing of instruments for this study, this researcher performed a Varimax factor analysis using the dataset from this study only (Kraft, N=140). This analysis yielded only two factors which accounted for a total of 49.15% of the variance. The Eigenvalues for the two factors were: factor 1 = 14.01 (38.91% of the variance) and factor 2 = 3.69 (10.24% of the variance).

Factor 1 consists of 28 items that deal with many task- and performance-associated behaviors, as well as the team leader's interpersonal interaction with his/her team members. This factor 1 is identified as a general leadership orientation toward empowering others, i.e., "empowered leadership." Factor 2 consists of eight items that may represent an underlying dimension related to "old" traditional leader behaviors (i.e., revealing rigid, inflexible behaviors). The following items seem to relate to the inability to adapt to a changing environment: #1. Keep information to myself, #2. Make decisions for the team, #3. Stick to the original plan, #4. Focus on one side of the issue, #5. Handle only one assignment at a time, #6. Neglect to communicate, and #7. Overlook opportunities to coordinate activities between teams. This inability to adapt was likely, because the organization was only one year into the evolution toward teams. A reasonable label for factor 2 is "traditional leadership." The factor loadings are shown in table 4.4.

It is noteworthy that seven of the eight items comprising factor 2 had reversed scoring on the instrument. Thus, it is possible that the appearance of these two factors, one consisting solely of positively worded items and the other consisting almost entirely of negatively worded items, is no more than an unexpected result of the instrument construction. In that case, one could not correctly conclude that two clear and different content dimensions exist.

Table 4.3: Rotated Factor Analysis of Combined Data of SMT

ITEM	Loading		
	F1	**F2**	**F3**
Improve the way the team operates	.88	.17	.26
Encourage team members to develop new skills	.87	.08	.25
Encourage team members to monitor their own performance	.86	.02	.35
Respond to unanticipated changes	.86	.02	.40
Work through conflicts	.86	.08	.38
Observe my own behaviors	.85	.16	.28
Am able to present alternative ideas to team members	.84	.20	.29
Communicate my thoughts clearly	.83	.19	.31
Develop solutions that capitalize on the differences among team members	.83	.16	.24
Pay attention to detail	.80	.17	.24
Attend to nonverbal cues	.80	-.05	.32
Develop a climate of personal growth for team members	.77	.34	.15
Give feedback to team members	.77	.22	.24
Help teams to meet schedule requirements	.76	.33	.06
Anticipate potential problems for the team	.74	.35	.08
Neglect to communicate customer requirements	.69	-.01	.56
Overlook opportunities to coordinate activities between teams	.68	-.06	.57
Cope with uncertainty	.63	.46	.11
Rely on the most knowledgeable team members for input	.57	-.25	.56
Encourage team members to manage themselves	.46	.45	24

Table 4.3 (continued)

ITEM	Loading		
	F1	**F2**	**F3**
Encourage open communication among team members	-.19	.82	-.04
Foster smooth team interaction	.29	.77	.04
Develop a climate of team work	.29	.75	-.11
Address interpersonal problems on a one-on-one basis	.21	-.72	.20
Identify problems teams are avoiding	.15	.70	-.11
Listen to team members	.25	.69	.26
Am able to change course to take advantage of opportunities	.37	.66	.00
Influence people to follow the rules	.49	-.54	.44
Make decisions for the team	.20	-.02	.83
Focus on one side of an issue	.44	.17	.73
Stick to the original plan when the unexpected occurs	.31	-.33	.70
Can handle only one assignment at a time	.60	-.01	.66

PHASE 2: CORRELATIONAL ANALYSIS

The second research question was stated as follows: Is there a relationship between team leadership skills and team performance? This question was examined using correlational analysis between team leadership assessment data and team performance data. The two instruments, Team Leader Survey (TLS) and the SMT Leader Survey, were each correlated with performance data collected at two separate time periods. Additionally, each item and each of the originally proposed dimensions were correlated with the performance data collected at two separate time periods.

Table 4.4: Factor Analysis (SMT—Kraft dataset only)

Item	Loading	
	F1	**F2**
Encourage open communication among team members	.77	-.09
Identify problems teams are avoiding	.67	-.03
Obtain resources for team members	.71	.03
Develop a climate of teamwork	.80	.05
Foster smooth team interaction	.83	-.10
Change course to take advantage of opportunities	.76	-.01
Listen to team members	.76	-.21
Solve team problems on my own	.57	.33
Establish priorities for the team	-.70	-.17
Encourage team members to manage themselves	.55	-.07
Address interpersonal problems on a one-to-one basis	-.71	-.03
Cope with uncertainty	.67	.03
Anticipate potential problems for the team	.74	.02
Help teams to meet schedule requirements	.78	.04
Develop a climate of personal growth for team members	.71	.07
Give feedback to team members	.61	-.14
Pay attention to detail	.73	-.04
Influence people to follow the rules	-.65	-.13
Develop solutions that capitalize on the differences among team members	.68	.06
Present alternative ideas to team members	.77	-.08
Communicate thoughts clearly	.77	.00
Observe own behaviors	.73	.09
Improve the way the team operates	.81	.13
Encourage team members to develop new skills	.64	.06
Attend to nonverbal cues	.32	.17
Encourage team members to monitor own performance	.57	.02
Work through conflicts	.69	.00
Respond to unanticipated changes	.70	-.05
Keep information to myself	-.02	-.57
Make decisions for the team	-.29	-.63
Stick to the original plan when the unexpected occurs	-.33	-.65
Focus on one side of an issue	.18	-.79
Rely on the most knowledgeable team members for input	-.15	-.48
Can handle only one assignment at a time	.19	-.71
Neglect to communicate customer requirements	.16	-.61
Overlook opportunities to coordinate activities between teams	.13	-.70

Note: Factor 1 may be identified as empowered leadership. Factor 2 may be identified as traditional leadership.

Correlational Analysis for the Team Leader Survey (TLS)

A Pearson product moment correlation and a Spearman rank-order correlation were performed using the Team Leader Survey and performance data generated for two time periods which measured attainment of performance goals. The Pearson product moment correlation is the most commonly used index of relationships between two variables. The Spearman correlation is an appropriate alternative for use with ordinal data which may be ranked in two ordered series (Siegel, 1956). Time 1 (T1) was the week of March 3, 1995; time 2 (T2) was the week of April 28, 1995. Each time period had two sets of performance data. The first was based on BRP (business resources planning) performance metrics, and the second was based on BPCS (business planning and control system) performance metrics. These data are shown in tables 4.5, 4.6, 4.7, 4.8 and 4.9. Complete data are in Appendix E.

Table 4.5: Variables in the Analysis—Descriptive Statistics

Variable	Var. Label	N	Mean	Std. Dev.
TLS	Team Leader's total score	9	107.62	11.67
Factor 1	Team Leadership	9	61.57	7.90
Factor 2	Team Leader Learning	9	25.43	2.35
Time 1	T1 BRP Performance	7	86.43	14.18
Time 1	T1 BPCS Performance	6	94.33	11.50
Time 2	T2 BRP Performance	7	81.57	25.34
Time 2	T2 BPCS Performance	6	103.00	11.14

Note: The TLS survey was administered once; the performance data were collected twice.

None of the Pearson correlations were significant at the .05 level. The probabilities shown for the t-values are two-sided tests. It is possible that the extreme fluctuations in the BPCS coefficients from T1 to T2 may be due to random error variance or the small sample size.

Table 4.6: Pearson Correlation for the TLS with the Performance Data

Time 1 (*N* = 9)

		BRP			BPCS	
		BRP			**BPCS**	
Total TLS	.25	p = .59	t = .57	.51	p = .30	t = 1.19
TLS Dimensions:						
Factor 1: Leadership	.32	p = .49	t = .75	.47	p = .35	t = 1.06
Factor 2: Learning	-.14	p = .76	t = .32	.29	p = .57	t = .61

No significant relationships exist at the .05 level.

Table 4.7: Pearson Correlation for the TLS with the Performance Data

Time 2 (*N* = 9)

		BRP			**BPCS**	
Total TLS	.07	p = .88	t = .16	-.49	p = .32	t = 1.14
TLS Dimensions:						
Factor 1: Leadership	.11	p = .81	t = .25	-.64	p = .17	t = 1.66
Factor 2: Learning	-.18	p = .70	t = .41	.33	p = .52	t = .70

No significant relationships exist at the .05 level.

Table 4.8: Spearman Correlation of TLS Survey Data with Performance Data

Time 1 (*N* = 9)

	BRP		**BPCS**	
TLS Total	.21	t = .47	.26	t = .53
TLS Dimensions:				
Factor 1: Leadership	.21	t = .47	.09	t = .17
Factor 2: Learning	-.24	t = .56	.14	t = .29

* p<.05

Table 4.9: Spearman Correlation of TLS Survey Data with Performance Data

Time 2 (N = 9)

	Correlation with:			
	BRP		**BPCS**	
TLS Total	-.19	t = .43	-.43	t = .95
TLS Dimensions:				
Factor 1: Leadership	-.19	t = .43	-.43	t = .95
Factor 2: Learning	-.71*	t = 2.23	.00	t = .00

* p<.05

One of the Spearman correlations was significant at the .05 level. The team leader's own learning score is significant with the time 2 (T2) BRP production score. This correlation, however, is opposite to prediction. A possible explanation for this result is that it may be due to random error variance, the small sample size or some combination of these factors.

Correlational Analysis for SMT Leader Survey

A Pearson product moment correlation and a Spearman rank-order correlation were performed using the SMT and performance data generated for two time periods. The same data and time periods were used for this analysis as were used for the TLS. These data are shown in tables 4.10, 4.11, 4.12, 4.13, and 4.14.

Table 4.10: Variables in the Analysis—Descriptive Statistics

Variable	Var. Label	N	Mean	Std. Dev.
SMT	Team Leader's Total Score	9	126.07	5.96
Factor 1	Empowered Leadership	9	100.71	6.09
Factor 2	Traditional Leadership	9	25.35	2.68
Time 1	T1 BRP Performance	7	86.42	14.17
Time 1	T1 BPCS Performance	6	94.33	11.50
Time 2	T2 BRP Performance	7	81.57	25.33
Time 2	T2 BPCS Performance	6	103.00	11.13

Note. The SMT survey was administered once; the performance data were collected twice.

Table 4.11: Pearson Correlation for the SMT with the Performance Data

Time 1 (*N*=9)

		BRP			BPCS	
		Correlation with:				
Total SMT	.56	p = .19	t = 1.50	.12	p = .82	t = .24
SMT Dimensions:						
Factor 1: Empowered Leadership	.53	p = .22	t = 1.39	.37	p = .47	t = .80
Factor 2: Traditional Leadership	-.12	p = .80	t = .27	72*	p = .05	t = 2.09

*p<.05

Table 4.12: Pearson Correlation for the SMT with the Performance Data

Time 2 (N=9)

		BRP			BPCS	
		Correlation with:				
Total SMT	.33	p = .47	t =.79	-.49	p = .33	t = 1.12
SMT Dimensions:						
Factor 1: Empowered Leadership	.33	p = .47	t = .78	-.48	p = .33	t =1.10
Factor 2: Traditional Leadership	-.13	p = .78	t = .29	-.17	p = .74	t =.35

No significant relationships exist at the .05 level.

It is possible that the fluctuations in the BPCS coefficient from T1 to T2 may be due to random error variance or the small sample size.

Table 4.13: Spearman Correlation of SMT Survey Data with Production Data

Time 1 (N=9)

	Correlation with:			
	BRP		BPCS	
Total SMT	.51	t = 1.32	.37	t = .80
SMT Dimensions				
Factor 1: Empowered Leadership	.35	t = .83	.09	t = .17
Factor 2: Traditional Leadership	-.03	t = .06	-.83*	t = 2.96

*p<.05.

Table 4.14: Spearman Correlation of SMT Survey Data with Production Data

Time 2 (N=9)

	Correlation with:			
	BRP		BPCS	
Total SMT	.62	t = 1.75	-.43	t = .80
SMT Dimensions				
Factor 1: Empowered Leadership	.35	t = .83	-.29	t = .60
Factor 2: Traditional Leadership	.15	t = .34	.00	t = .00

No significant relationships exist at the .05 level.

TLS and SMT Item and Dimension Correlation With Performance Data

Although it was not possible to confirm the six proposed dimensions of either the TLS or the SMT, an analysis of each item and each of the initially proposed dimensions on each survey was performed and a Pearson correlation was administered to explain the significance of any specific question or dimension. Table 4.15 is a subset of the data that show the results of those items and dimensions that proved significant at the .05 level. Complete data are in Appendix E.

Table 4.15: Subset of TLS and SMT Item and Dimension

Pearson Correlations

Item	T1BRP		T1BPCS		T2BRP		T2BPCS	
	r	t	r	t	r	t	r	t
TLS Items								
Clearly defined role relationships with team members	-0.74	2.47						
Cooperate effectively with leaders and members of other teams			-0.99	18.1				
Help team members learn to work together better as a team	-0.74	2.49						
Help team members learn to adjust to changes in the team's organization			-0.92	4.83				
Team members understand what it means to be a self-managing team							0.84	3.04
Learning and using time management techniques							0.82	2.86
Learning to manage difficult people assertively							0.97	7.7
Developing and using new systems and procedures to improve my technical expertise							0.77	2.38
Learning from trial and error experiences			0.80	2.62				
Dimensions								
Leadership			-0.75	0.23				
Coping							0.90	4.19
SMT								

Table 4.15 (continued)

Item	T1BRP	T1BPCS	T2BRP	T2BPCS
Keep information to myself		0.87 3.57		
Anticipate potential problems for the team				0.97 7.7
Develop solutions that capitalize on differences among team members		-0.99 18.10		
Attend to nonverbal cues				-0.93 5.25
Overlook opportunities to coordinate activities between teams				0.84 3.04
Encourage team members to monitor their own performance	-0.84 3.52			
Respond to unanticipated changes	-0.74 2.47			
Dimensions				
Thinking		-0.75 2.30		

Note. All correlations shown are significant p<.05.

Tests Using High-Low Performance

In order to examine the differences in the teams' survey scores, the teams were divided into high- and low-performing teams based upon the performance data (BRP and BPCS) collected for both time periods (T1 and T2) combined to form a single score. Using the mean of the performance scores to separate high-performing teams from low-performing teams, the high-performing teams scored 89.5% or higher on combined performance measures of BRP and BPCS, while the low-performing teams scored lower than 89.5%. Complete data are in Appendix E.

A t-test was calculated to see if the TLS and SMT scores were different between the high-performing teams and the low-performing teams. Tables 4.16, 4.17, and 4.18 present the results of the t-tests.

Table 4.16: T-test for Combined Performance Measures (Production)

	Mean Diff.	DF	t-value	p-value
High-Low Teams	26.25	7	2.63	.03

Table 4.17: T-test for Team Leader Survey (TLS)

	Mean Diff.	DF	t-value	p-value
Team Leaders Total Score	10.13	7	1.28	24
Factor 1: Leadership	7.59	7	1.45	.19
Factor 2: Learning	.52	7	.29	.78

Table 4.18: T-test for Self-Managing Team (SMT) Leader Survey

	Mean Diff.	DF	t-value	p-value
Team Leaders Total Score	9.39	7	1.24	.26
Factor 1: Empowered Leadership	8.16	7	1.72	.13
Factor 2: Traditional Leadership	-.88	7	-.53	.61

The t-test results indicate that the performance (production) measurements of the two groups are significantly different. However, the results of the t-tests for the two survey instruments did not indicate a significant difference in scores on the team leadership measures.

Background Information

Although the original research plan did not include document analysis, the researcher did examine production and staffing records. It was determined that the productivity of this research site had increased dramatically since the implementation of self-managing work teams.

Historical document analysis consisted of reviewing personnel staffing records from 1993 to June 1995 and production records from 1993 to June 1995, and provided data in Tables 4.19, 4.20, and 4.21.

Table 4.19: Staffing

Date-Mo./Yr.	Full Time Employees	Temporary Employees	Total Staffing
12/93	150	13	163
12/94	140.5	32	172.5
6/95	146.5	54	200.5

Note. Staffing increased a total of 23% over an 18-month time period.

Table 4.20: Production Volume

Time Period	Number of Units Produced
January-April 1993	581,987 units
January-April 1994	869,684 units
January-April 1995	2,061,056 units

Note. Production volume increased by 254% over a 30-month period.

Table 4.21: Productivity Ratio

	1993	1994	1995
Units Produced	581,987	869,684	2,061,056
No. Employees	163.0	172.5	200.5
Units per Employee	3,570	5,042	10,280

Note: Productivity increased over a three-year period as shown above. The planning for self-managing teams took place in 1993, with full implementation in early 1994. Data collection for this study occurred in early 1995.

SUMMARY OF RESULTS

The results of the factor analysis of both instruments, the TLS and the SMT Leader Survey, resulted in the identification of two factors for each instrument. Both surveys identified one major factor which can best be described as a general leadership orientation toward empowering others. This was the primary factor identified in each survey instrument. The other distinguishable factors were the team leader's own learning strategies and a more traditional leadership factor.

The research hypothesis was that a positive relationship exists between the degree of team leader skills and team performance. The following results were obtained: (1) Two significant relationships were identified from the correlation of survey factors and the performance data, specifically, the team leader's learning strategies and the BRP performance data of time 2, and the traditional leadership orientation and the BPCS performance data of time 1. (Note, however, that these relationships were opposite what was predicted.) (2) Three of the original survey scales proved significant at the .05 level, specifically, leadership, coping and thinking skills. (3) Nine individual questions on the TLS were significantly related to the performance data when both time periods and both measures (BRP and BPCS) were combined. (4) Seven individual questions on the SMT Leader survey were significantly related to performance data when both time periods and both measures (BRP and BPCS) were combined. (5) Significant differences were found between high- and low-performing teams on the performance measures, but not on the survey scores for either TLS or SMT (using the two factors of each, not items or dimensions).

An analyses of production records and personnel staffing records cast some light on the production environment in which the self-managing teams were working. Historical document analysis revealed that during the 18 months preceding this study, production volume increased 137% while staffing increased only 23%.

This chapter has presented the data analyses results. The following chapter will focus on conclusions and how these findings relate to previous research, implications for organizations and recommendations for future research.

CHAPTER 5

Conclusions and Recommendations

This chapter presents the conclusions of the study. First, the study is summarized, with discussion incorporating the study's findings and comparing them to theories reported in the literature. Second, the limitations of this study are discussed. Third, the future implications of team leadership training and development are explored. Fourth, directions for future research are suggested.

SUMMARY AND FINDINGS OF THE STUDY

The central purpose of this study was to investigate the relationship between team leadership and team performance. Because these concepts are of current interest to many individuals in organizations, numerous theorists and practitioners have written about these concepts, but they have not adequately tested them. Specifically, this study explored three areas: (1) the relationship between team leadership and team performance, (2) the necessary skills and behaviors of team leaders, and (3) the development of a survey instrument to assess team leadership.

The development of an instrument to assess team leader behavior was included in this study because no fully developed instrument existed. As noted earlier, the SMT Leader Survey instrument was still in development at the beginning of this study. Data obtained from the responses to the survey instrument were subjected to statistical evaluation.

Participants in this study consisted of 140 members of a small manufacturing plant of a midsize pharmaceutical company in the northeastern United States. From the population of 140, a subset of 118 team members assessed nine team leaders who all represented the first level of management in the organization and were external leaders of the teams. The SMT Leader Survey and the Team Leader Survey (TLS) were used to assess team leader skills and behaviors. Consistent measures of productivity were used for all teams.

MAJOR FINDINGS

There were three major findings in this study. The findings and their importance will be presented in this section.

Identification of Team Leader Skills and Behaviors

The first major finding is that the primary aspect of team leadership can be seen as a single broad category of behavior definable as a general orientation toward empowering others. This finding is supported by factor analyses of both survey instruments. While Burress (1992, 1993, 1994) and Glaser (1991, 1992) had each suggested six somewhat different dimensions of team leadership, this study found it impossible to define the concept of team leadership in six distinguishable factors. The general orientation toward empowering others included items which focused on self-management, leadership, empowerment, and facilitating the learning of team members.

This finding supports the work of Manz and Sims (1987) and their position that the role of the external team leader is to encourage and facilitate their employees to use self-managing behaviors. Interestingly, Manz' and Sims' original factor analysis of their 1987 study revealed one large factor and five much smaller factors (Glaser, 1992). Finally, these findings support the work of Sims and Lorenzi (1992) when they state that the development of employee self-management is the new leadership paradigm.

Traditional Leadership and Managerial Skills

The second major finding is that the factor analysis of the SMT leader survey revealed a factor which appears to reflect traditional leadership and managerial skills. This finding is important because it suggests that traditional leadership concepts continue to play an important role during the transition to self-managing teams and in relation to the team's performance. In other words, while the concepts of empowered leadership are important, it appears that traditional leadership concepts may be important, too, at least during the first year of the transition to self-managed teams at this site. The teams in this study were surveyed at the one-year point in their development. It is not possible to speculate beyond the one-year point concerning the value of traditional leadership concepts based upon the data in this study. However, this finding may support Sashkin's (1985) viewpoint that it is important for a good leader to be both a visionary (transformational) leader and a traditional (transactional) leader. Later, Sashkin and Rosenbach, further stated this position: " . . . transformational leaders use transactional, managerial roles not simply to define, assign, and accomplish tasks and achieve goals but also to educate, empower, and ultimately transform followers" (1993, p. 20). This study's results may very well support that viewpoint.

Team Leadership and Team Performance

The third major finding is that the concept of empowered leadership is not significantly correlated with the team performance data. Thus, it is not possible to reject the null hypothesis. In fact, the two survey factors which were significantly related to team performance were the traditional leadership factor and the team leader's learning strategy. Moreover, the latter factor was shown to have a negative relationship with performance. One possible explanation for this may be that the team members in this study were not aware of the learning strategies of their team leaders.

These findings highlight the difficulty in linking leadership with group performance. While teams are an increasingly popular approach to organizing and managing work, there has been difficulty in demonstrating that the use of teams improves productivity. This study's finding supports Hackman's (1990) challenge of traditional models of group effectiveness in which specific causes are tightly linked to performance outcomes. He states that:

> Influences on group effectiveness do not come in separate, easily distinguishable packages. They come, instead, in complex tangles that often are as hard to straighten out as a backlash on a fishing reel. To try to sort out the effects of each possible determinant of team effectiveness can lead to the conclusion that no single factor has a very powerful effect—a conclusion reached by more than one reviewer of the group performance literature. Each possible cause

loses its potency when examined in isolation from other conditions also in place for the groups under study (p. 8).

The additional background data analysis in this study also sheds light on the productivity aspect of teams. This analysis clearly shows a dramatic increase in this manufacturing plant's overall productivity. Though there continues to be difficulty in demonstrating that the use of teams improves productivity, it is important to consider the overall environment in which the teams are operating. In this study, the fact that production volume increased dramatically soon after the reorganization to teams most likely contributed to an unstable environment. Replication of this study at the two-year or three-year anniversary of the implementation of teams would have probably provided better results due to a more stable environment.

Social scientists have realized for many years that human behavior can best be understood by examining many variables at the same time. The reality of complex social institutions calls out for researchers to examine many variables simultaneously (McMillan & Schumacher, 1989).

However, the reality of field research is that one can rarely control multiple variables. The researcher is often reduced to conducting simple experimental studies investigating the effect of one variable on another using correlational analysis. These procedures, however, fail to reflect researchers' current understanding of the multiplicity of factors at play in organizations and in human behavior in general.

Limitations

This study reveals overall weak relationships between team leadership skills and team performance. Several explanations for this result are possible. In this study, the sample size was especially small when the original 11 teams used in the factor analysis were reduced to only nine after two teams were eliminated due to a lack of performance data. This was disappointing, but not unusual. Other researchers have also noted that it is sometimes impossible to use objective, group-level performance data for all groups in the sample (Cohen, 1993).

Another factor affecting this study was the low variability in survey scores among the team leaders. Additionally, the lowest scoring team leader on both surveys had no production data and was eliminated. The team leaders were tightly clustered in their total scores on both survey instruments.

Still another critical factor affecting this study was the measurement method of team performance at the research site. Team performance metrics were initiated in January 1995 (the year of data collection). Prior year records were maintained by functional department. During 1995, each team's performance was measured according to percentage attainment of goal. Many of the goals were 100% attained. This method did not account for the large increase in the production volume from the previous year. By simply stating 100% attainment of goal, for example, it was impossible for the researcher to ascertain whether this was a "stretch" goal for the team, or a "low ceiling" goal. This researcher discovered the impact of this type measurement when reviewing historical records concerning production volume and personnel staffing levels.

A final point to consider is that the two survey instruments used to assess team leadership are new and are still being evaluated and revised. Specifically, the TLS has not been tested beyond the organization used in the current study. Furthermore, because the survey instruments were administered in only one organization for this study, the generalizability of the findings is limited.

Implications for Team Leader Training and Development

The implications for team leader training and development are of primary interest to practitioners. As researchers better define the necessary skills and behaviors of team leaders in self-managing team environments, the organizational development and training practitioners may use this information to develop more effective training programs and developmental activities. In fact, any manager who must select, train, counsel, and evaluate team leaders could benefit from information focused on developing this unique type of leader.

This study's results may suggest the need for both empowering leadership behaviors as well as more traditional leadership behaviors in team leaders who are in a transition mode. This supports Glaser's (1992) contention that leadership behavior occurs along a continuum where team leaders relinquish aspects of control to the teams only when they are ready to receive it. It is unclear whether or not this blend of leadership skills is a temporary need during the first year of transition to teams at this site, or if it is ongoing.

While it is clear from these results that developing the team to become fully self-managing is important and is future-focused, equally important is a present-day focus in managing the transition. This is of major importance to organizational practitioners who are charged with the responsibility of instructional design and training. Caution is advised in eliminating all traditional leadership concepts in favor of the newer empowered leadership concepts. A balance of both appears to be needed. As Nadler (1995) states:

> Probably 15% of managers are natural team leaders; another 15% could never lead a team because it runs counter to their personality. Then there's that huge group in the middle. Team leadership doesn't come naturally to them, but they can learn it (p. 100).

Appropriate training methods should also be a consideration. Training methods suited to adult learners would be especially effective. Methods that are active and trainee-centered, such as case study and behavior modeling, seem appropriate for this learning environment. Such methods complement the more traditional training methods, such as classroom and lecture, that are best suited for instructing trainees on other concepts.

In particular, behavior modeling has merit in the team leader training context. Behavior modeling, a learning process involving imitating others' behaviors, is based on Bandura's observational learning model (Bandura, 1969). Researchers have documented the effectiveness of employee training programs that involve the imitation of behavior models (Latham & Saari, 1979). These types of training programs make extensive use of behavior models via videotaped role playing. In addition, Mezirow's (1990) *Fostering Critical Reflection in Adulthood* reviews exemplary programs and suggests methods for fostering transformative learning in the workplace.

Self-directed learning should also be encouraged among team leaders. Continual employee learning is becoming a way of organizational life. As such, team leaders should be responsible for assessing their own learning needs and initiating action to meet those needs. Self-directed learning should increase team leaders' acceptance of training content as well as transfer the training from the classroom to the work setting. Other forms of self-directed learning may involve independent study, such as reading a book or seeking informal mentors in the organization.

Creation of a noncompetitive work environment among the team leaders should be established. Weekly team leader meetings could be established for the purpose of sharing learnings, providing support for one another, and engaging in dialogue sessions with the aim of enhancing the level of communication and meaning of the team leader experience.

Suggestions for Future Research

Not surprisingly, this research site was a manufacturing facility. The genesis of many employee-involvement practices is in manufacturing settings, where trends such as new plant designs (Lawler, 1978), sociotechnical systems work design (Pasmore, 1978), quality circles, and many Total Quality Management (TQM) practices were initiated. Lawler et al. (1995) report that U.S. manufacturing employees are the most extensively covered by employee-involvement practices, including self-managing teams. Future research of this study type is needed in nonmanufacturing organizations in order to explore the applicability of self-managing teams in knowledge work settings.

It is clear that better instruments are needed to assess team leadership. The TLS and SMT leader survey instruments would benefit from additional examination and development because both appear to be potentially important instruments that measure a broad aspect defined as a leadership orientation toward empowering others. Both instruments need to be tested more extensively and in other organizations.

More research needs to be done on the causal relationships between team leadership and other independent, mediating, and moderating variables that determine team performance. Because team leadership appears to be a critical element in the development and success of self-managing teams, additional research could provide information critical to the selection, training and development of future team leaders.

Replication of this study in other organizations would provide more information on the generalizability of the findings. Additional research on the general question of the efficacy of self-managing teams is needed. In the meantime, organizations should proceed cautiously when implementing self-managing teams, using sound principles and theories to guide the initiatives.

Conclusions

Thus far, the growth in the adoption of teams has outpaced the ability of theory and research to provide solid underpinnings for sound practices, although this gap is narrowing. However, this researcher is convinced that teams, in some form, will survive for many years to come. Additionally, teams will continue to evolve as the years unfold and as practitioners and researchers continue to learn. In the meantime, perhaps Lewin's famous line is still right on target . . . "there is nothing so practical as a good theory" (Marrow, 1969). Organizations may be guided in the development of self-managing teams by the theories presented in this study, especially those of Bandura, Manz and Sims, and Mezirow.

Perhaps Hackman (1990) best sums up the potential of teams:

> The comparative advantage of a team is not in simple execution of the work. It is, instead, in a team's flexibility, adaptability, diversity (for example, in member knowledge, skill, and experience), and capability to learn and change over time. Teams, when they work, are flexible, adaptive, and capable of collective learning (p. 474).

This researcher agrees with this assessment of teams' potential. Moreover, to provide conditions in which individuals and teams can develop their capacity to learn and create an organization that they care about, organizational leaders must invest time and money far beyond what most consider appropriate today. A willingness to invest in creating an environment that helps employees learn and develop is essential to success.

Appendices

APPENDIX A: DESCRIPTIVE STATISTICS OF TEAMS

Table A-1: Description of All Team Members Only

Respondents	N	Mdn.	Mode	Other Comments
Seniority	118	12 mos.	68% = 12 months	
Age	118	38.7 yrs.	26.3% = 30-39 & 26.3% = 40-49	
Ethnic	118		56% White	15% Asian 14% Black 7% Hispanic 7% Other 1% No Answer
Education	118		29% Some College	20% High School 24% Bachelors 23% Masters
Sex	118		50% Male	49% Female 1% No Answer

Note. 118 members of nine teams

APPENDIX B: TEAM LEADER SURVEY (TLS)

Team Leader Survey - Self Evaluation

Please complete the following information:

Your Name _____

Name of Your Team _____

Length of Time on this Team ___ months

Age: ___ less than 20

          ___ 20–29

          ___ 30–39

          ___ 40–49

          ___ 50–59

          ___ 60 or over

Sex: ___ male ___ female

Indicate your highest education level completed:

          ____ less than high school graduate

          ____ high school graduate

          ____ some college

          ____ college graduate - bachelor's degree

          ____ college graduate - master's degree

          ____ college graduate - doctorate

Directions: On the following pages, you will find a list of 31 behaviors. Read each statement carefully and decide to what extent you display each of the behaviors described. Indicate your response by circling the letter(s) on the Response Form that corresponds to your choice. Use the following key:

VG   = To a Very Great Extent
G   = To a Great Extent
M   = To a Moderate Extent
S   = To a Slight Extent
L   = To Little or No Extent

Team Leader Survey - Self Evaluation

1. I have clearly defined role relationships with team members.
2. I cooperate effectively with leaders and members of other teams.
3. I help team members take responsibility for the team's work.
4. I help team members learn to work together better as a team.
5. I help team members learn to work together better interpersonally.
6. I help team members learn to plan their activities. (Including setting goals and organizing their work.)
7. I help team members learn how to implement group tasks effectively.
8. I help team members learn how to communicate better through formal and informal meetings.
9. I help team members learn how to solve problems as a group.
10. I help team members learn how to make decisions as a group.
11. I help team members learn how to resolve their own conflicts and disagreements.
12. I help team members learn how to check and, when necessary, correct their own work.
13. I help team members learn how to reinforce effective team behaviors.
14. I help team members learn to discipline themselves.
15. I help team members learn to select new colleagues.
16. I help team members learn to adjust to changes in the team's organization.
17. I help team members learn how to get the job skills needed to get the team's job done.
18. I help team members learn how to get the self-managing team skills needed to work together effectively.
19. I help team members understand what it means to be a self-managing team.
20. I help team members learn to think for themselves.

Concerning your development as a team leader, to what extent do you use each of the following strategies:

21. Learning and using time management techniques.
22. Learning and using stress management techniques.
23. Learning to manage difficult people assertively.
24. Developing and using new systems and procedures to improve my technical expertise.
25. Developing and using new team process facilitation skills.
26. Learning through formal training experiences.
27. Informal learning from my colleagues.
28. Learning from other team members.
29. Learning by reading on my own.
30. Learning from mentors.
31. Learning from trial and error experiences.

Thank you for completing this survey.

Team Member Form of Team Leader Survey

Please complete the following information:

Name of Your Team _____

Length of Time on this Team _____ months

Age: ___ less than 20

         ___ 20–29

         ___ 30–39

         ___ 40–49

         ___ 50–59

         ___ 60 or over

Sex: _____ male ___ female

Indicate your highest education level completed:

         _____ less than high school graduate

         _____ high school graduate

         _____ some college

         _____ college graduate - bachelor's degree

_____ college graduate - master's degree

_____ college graduate - doctorate

Your relationship to the team leader of this team (check one):

_____Team Member   _____ Other (please define)

Directions: Read each statement carefully and decide to what extent this person (team leader) displays the behavior described. Indicate your response by circling the letter (s) on the Response Form that corresponds to your choice. Use the following key in determining your responses:

VG = To a Very Great Extent
G   = To a Great Extent
M   = To a Moderate Extent
S   = To a Slight Extent
L   = To Little or No Extent

Team Leader Survey - Feedback

When working with a self-managing team, this person . . .

1. Clearly defines role relationships with team members.

2. Cooperates effectively with leaders and members of other teams.

3. Helps team members take responsibility for the team's work.

4. Helps team members learn to work together better as a team.

5. Helps team members learn to work together better interpersonally.

6. Helps team members learn to plan their activities. (Including setting goals and organizing our work.)

7. Helps team members learn how to implement group tasks effectively.

8. Helps team members learn how to communicate better through formal and informal meetings.

9. Helps team members learn how to solve problems as a group.

10. Helps team members learn how to make decisions as a group.

11. Helps team members learn how to resolve their own conflicts and disagreements.

12. Helps team members learn how to check and, when necessary, correct their own work.

13. Helps team members learn how to reinforce effective team behaviors.

14. Helps team members learn how to discipline themselves.

15. Helps team members learn to select new colleagues.

16. Helps team members learn to adjust to changes in the team's organization.

17. Helps team members learn how to get the job skills needed to get the team's job done.

18. Helps team members learn how to get the self-managing team skills needed to work together effectively.

19. Helps team members understand what it means to be a self-managing team.

20. Helps team members learn to think for themselves.

Concerning his/her own development as a team leader, to what extent does this person use each of the following strategies:

21. Learning and using time management techniques.

22. Learning and using stress management techniques.

23. Learning to manage difficult people assertively.

24. Developing and using new systems and procedures to improve his/her own technical expertise.

25. Developing and using new team process facilitation skills.

26. Learning from formal training experiences.

27. Informal learning from colleagues.

28. Learning from other team members.

29. Learning from reading on his/her own.

30. Learning from mentors.

31. Learning from trial and error experiences.

Thank you for completing this survey.

APPENDIX C: RELIABILITY DATA

Table C-1: Instrument Reliability—Cronbach's Alpha

TLS Instrument	
All Items	0.97
Factors 1 & 2 only	0.97
SMT Instrument	
SMT all items	0.95

APPENDIX D: SURVEY DATA AND PERFORMANCE DATA

Table D-1: Survey Scores and Performance Data

Name (case)	TLS Total Score	Factor 1: Team Leadership	Factor 2 Learning	T1 BRP Production Data	T1 BPCS Production Data	T2 BRP Production Data	T2 BPCS Production Data
Team Leader 1 (TL1)	101.00	56.75	25.25	58	—	26	—
TL2	107.67	63.08	24.17	—	100	—	100
TL3	117.36	67.68	26.77	—	100	—	100
TL4	89.09	50.64	20.91	100	—	100	—
TL5	128.39	75.39	28.67	97	98	86	93
TL6	102.20	58.00	25.20	85	71	84	100
TL7	99.40	54.80	24.80	84	—	94	—
TL8	107.00	58.60	58.40	85	100	84	125
TL9	116.44	69.22	24.67	96	97	97	100

Table D-1 (continued)

Name (case)	SMT Total Score	Factor 1: Empowered Leadership	Factor 2: Traditional Leadership	T1 BRP Production Data	T1 BPCS Production Data	T2 BRP Production Data	T2 BPCS Production Data
Team Leader 1 (TL1)	122.88	95.13	27.75	58	—	26	—
TL2	118.42	197.17	21.25	—	100	—	100
TL3	125.55	103.41	22.14	—	100	—	100
TL4	125.55	96.27	29.27	100	—	100	—
TL5	138.33	113.61	24.72	97	98	86	93
TL6	123.60	96.60	27.00	85	71	84	100
TL7	125.80	99.00	26.80	84	—	94	—
TL8	122.00	98.60	23.40	85	100	84	125
TL9	132.56	106.67	25.89	96	97	97	100

APPENDIX E: STATISTICAL BACKGROUND DATA

Table E-1: Team Performance Measures

Team	T1	T2	Avg. Perf.	Hi-Lo Teams
1	58.00	26.00	42.00	Low
2	100.00	100.00	100.00	High
3	100.00	100.00	100.00	High
4	100.00	100.00	100.00	High
5	97.50	89.50	93.50	High
6	78.00	92.00	85.00	Low
7	84.00	94.00	89.00	Low
8	92.50	104.50	89,50	High
9	96.50	98.50	97.50	High
Measures				
Mean	89.61	89.39	98.50	
Std. Deviation	14.18	24.23	18.60	
Std. Error	4.73	8.08	6.20	
Variance	200.92	586.92	346.06	
Coeff. of Variation	.16	.27	.21	
Minimum	58.00	26.00	42.00	
Maximum	100.00	104.50	100.00	
Range	42.00	78.50	58.00	
Sum	806.50	804.50	805.50	
Sum of Squares	73878.75	76608.75	74860.75	

Note. T1 = time period one percentage of goal attainment; T2 = time period two percentage of goal attainment; Avg. = average of both time periods.

Table E-2: Supporting data for t-test for SMT

Team	SMT Total	F1	F2	Avg. Perf.	Hi-Lo Teams
1	122.88	95.13	27.75	42.00	Low
2	118.42	97.17	21.25	100.00	High
3	125.55	103.41	22.14	100.00	High
4	125.55	96.27	29.27	100.00	High
5	138.33	113.61	24.72	93.50	High
6	123.60	96.60	27.00	85.00	Low
7	125.80	99.00	26.80	89.00	Low
8	122.00	98.60	23.40	98.50	High
9	132.56	106.67	25.89	97.50	High
Measures					
Mean	126.08	100.72	25.36	89.50	
Std. Deviation	5.96	6.09	2.68	18.60	
Std. Error	1.99	2.03	.89	6.20	
Variance	35.56	37.11	7.20	346.06	
Coeff. of Variation	.05	.06	.11	.21	
Minimum	118.42	95.13	21.25	42.00	
Maximum	138.33	113.61	29.27	100.00	
Range	19.92	18.49	8.02	58.00	
Sum	1134.67	906.45	228.22	805.50	
Sum of Squares	143337.66	91591.93	5844.75	74860.75	

Note: F1 = factor 1; F2 = factor 2; Avg. Perf. = team average performance score for both time periods (percentage of goal attainment).

Table E-3: Supporting data for t-test for TLS

Team	TLS Total	F1	F2	Avg. Perf.	Hi-Lo Teams
1	101.00	56.75	25.25	42.00	Low
2	107.67	63.08	24.17	100.00	High
3	117.36	67.68	26.77	100.00	High
4	89.09	50.64	20.91	100.00	High
5	128.39	75.39	28.67	93.50	High
6	102.20	58.00	25.20	85.00	Low
7	99.40	54.80	24.80	89.00	Low
8	107.00	58.60	28.40	98.50	High
9	116.44	69.22	24.67	97.50	High
Measures					
Mean	107.62	61.57	25.43	89.50	
Std. Deviation	11.67	7.90	2.35	18.60	
Std. Error	3.89	2.63	.78	6.20	
Variance	136.07	62.40	5.52	346.06	
Coeff. of Variation	.11	.13	.09		
Minimum	89.09	50.64	20.91	42.00	
Maximum	128.39	75.39	28.67	100.00	
Range	39.30	24.75	7.76	58.00	
Sum	968.55	554.16	228.84	805.50	
Sum of Squares	105320.69	34620.70	5862.83	74860.75	

Note: F1 = factor 1; F2 = factor 2; Avg. perf. = team average performance score for both time periods (percentage of goal attainment).

Table E-4: Descriptive Statistics for Test Version of Team Leader Survey (TLS)

Item	Mean	S.D.
Clearly defines role relationships	3.56	0.53
Cooperates effectively with other teams	4.22	0.44
Helping team members take responsibility for team's work	4.00	0.50
Helping team members learn to work together better as a team	4.22	0.44
Helping team members learn to work together better interpersonally	3.67	0.71
Helping team members learn to plan their activities	3.33	0.71
Helping team members learn how to implement group tasks	3.67	1.00
Helping team members learn how to communicate better	3.78	0.67
Helping team members learn how to solve problems as a group	3.89	1.05
Helping team members learn how to make decisions as a group	3.78	0.97
Helping team members learn how to resolve own conflicts	3.33	1.12
Helping team members learn how to check and correct own work	3.78	0.83
Helping team members learn how to reinforce effective team behaviors	3.00	0.87
Helping team members learn how to discipline themselves	2.89	1.27
Helping team members learn how to select new colleagues	2.89	1.54
Helping team members learn how to adjust to changes	2.89	1.17
Helping team members learn how to get the job skills needed	3.33	0.71
Helping team members learn how to be self-managing	3.00	1.00
Helping team members understand what it means to be a self-managing team	4.00	0.71
Helping team members learn how to think for themselves	4.00	0.87
Learning and using time management	2.67	1.41
Learning and using stress management	2.22	1.30
Learning to manage difficult people assertively	3.22	0.44
Developing and using new systems and procedures to improve my own technical expertise	3.56	0.88

Appendices

Table E-4 (continued)

Item	Mean	S.D.
Developing and using new team process facilitation skills	3.22	0.83
Using what was learned from formal training experiences	3.33	0.87
Using informal learnings from colleagues	4.00	0.50
Using learnings from other team members	4.00	0.50
Using learnings from own reading	3.44	1.33
Using learnings from mentors	3.33	1.12
Using learnings from trial and error experiences	3.67	0.87
Dimension		
Leadership	7.78	0.83
Empowerment	11.89	1.05
Self-management	37.22	7.31
Coping	14.89	3.62
Learning-others	14.33	2.29
Learning-own	21.78	2.91
Total	107.89	14.27

Note: N=9 (9 teams = 118 members)

Table E-5: Correlations of Performance Measures With all Team Leader Survey (TLS) Items

Time 1

Item	Correlation with:					
	BRP			BPCS		
1	-0.74	p=0.06	t=2.47	-0.38	p=0.46	t=0.82
2	-0.09	p=0.84	t=0.20	-0.99	p=0.00	t=18.07
3	-0.04	p=0.92	t=0.10	0.00	p=1.00	t=0.00
4	-0.74	p=0.06	t=2.49	—	p=0.00	t=100.00
5	0.28	p=0.55	t=0.65	-0.44	p=0.38	t=0.99
6	0.36	p=0.43	t=0.86	-0.38	p=0.46	t=0.82
7	0.05	p=0.91	t=0.11	-0.46	p=0.36	t=1.03
8	0.45	p=0.31	t=1.14	-0.06	p=0.91	t=0.12
9	0.07	p=0.88	t=0.16	-0.32	p=0.54	t=0.67
10	-0.03	p=0.94	t=0.07	0.03	p=0.95	t=0.07
11	-0.17	p=0.72	t=0.38	-0.58	p=0.23	t=1.43
12	0.06	p=0.90	t=0.13	0.06	p=0.91	t=0.12
13	-0.08	p=0.87	t=0.17	-0.38	p=0.46	t=0.83
14	-0.12	p=0.79	t=0.28	-0.73	p=0.10	t=2.16
15	0.20	p=0.67	t=0.45	-0.41	p=0.42	t=0.90
16	-0.60	p=0.15	t=1.68	-0.92	p=0.01	t=4.83

Table E-5 (continued)

Item		BRP			BPCS	
					Correlation with:	
17	-0.04	p=0.92	t=0.10	-0.36	p=0.49	t=0.76
18	0.15	p=0.75	t=0.33	-0.55	p=0.26	t=1.30
19	-0.35	p=0.45	t=0.82	-0.02	p=0.98	t=0.03
20	0.33	p=0.46	t=0.79	0.02	p=0.97	t=0.04
21	-0.52	p=0.24	t=1.35	0.46	p=0.36	t=1.04
22	0.12	p=0.81	t=0.26	-0.56	p=0.25	t=1.35
23	-0.09	p=0.84	t=0.21	0.24	p=0.65	t=0.50
24	-0.31	p=0.49	t=0.74	0.19	p=0.72	t=0.39
25	-0.02	p=0.97	t=0.04	-0.51	p=0.31	t=1.17
26	-0.12	p=0.79	t=0.28	-0.29	p=0.58	t=0.61
27	—	p=0.00	t=100.00	0.00	p=1.00	t=0.00
28	-0.04	p=0.92	t=0.10	0.00	p=1.00	t=0.00
29	-0.03	p=0.95	t=0.07	0.71	p=0.11	t=2.04
30	0.54	p=0.21	t=1.44	-0.38	p=0.46	t=0.81
31	0.44	p=0.33	t=1.09	-0.80	p=0.06	t=2.62

Table E-6: Correlations of Performance Measures With All Team Leader Survey (TLS) Items

Time 2

Item	Correlation with:					
	BRP			BPCS		
1	-0.47	p=0.29	t=1.19	0.52	p=0.29	t=1.23
2	0.20	p=0.67	t=0.46	-0.13	p=0.80	t=0.27
3	0.04	p=0.93	t=0.09	0.71	p=0.11	t=2.02
4	-0.58	p=0.17	t=1.60	—	p=0.00	t=100.00
5	0.44	p=0.33	t=1.08	-0.52	p=0.29	t=1.23
6	0.63	p=0.13	t=1.83	0.52	p=0.29	t=1.23
7	0.08	p=0.87	t=0.17	-0.06	p=0.91	t=0.12
8	0.54	p=0.21	t=1.44	0.07	p=0.89	t=0.14
9	0.18	p=0.70	t=0.41	0.36	p=0.49	t=0.76
10	0.15	p=0.74	t=0.35	0.54	p=0.27	t=1.28
11	0.14	p=0.77	t=0.31	0.43	p=0.39	t=0.96
12	0.21	p=0.65	t=0.48	0.50	p=0.31	t=1.16
13	0.22	p=0.64	t=0.50	0.21	p=0.69	t=0.43
14	0.11	p=0.82	t=0.24	0.34	p=0.51	t=0.72
15	0.31	p=0.50	t=0.72	0.29	p=0.58	t=0.60
16	-0.40	p=0.37	t=0.98	-0.18	p=0.74	t=0.36
17	0.03	p=0.94	t=0.08	-0.29	p=0.58	t=0.60

Table E-6 (continued)

Item	Correlation with:					
	BRP			BPCS		
18	0.24	p=0.61	t=0.55	-0.06	p=0.91	t=0.12
19	-0.04	p=0.93	t=0.09	0.84	p=0.04	t-3.04
20	0.43	p=0.33	t=1.08	0.36	p=0.48	t=0.78
21	-0.53	p=0.22	t=1.42	0.82	p=0.05	t=2.86
22	0.36	p=0.43	t=0.86	0.66	p=0.15	t=1.75
23	0.20	p=0.67	t=0.46	0.97	p=0.00	t=7.70
24	-0.17	p=0.71	t=0.39	0.77	p=0.08	t=2.38
25	0.17	p=0.72	t=0.38	0.50	p=0.31	t=1.16
26	0.03	p=0.95	t=0.06	0.19	p=0.71	t=0.39
27	—	p=0.00	t=100.00	0.00	p=1.00	t=0.00
28	0.04	p=0.93	t=0.09	0.71	p=0.11	t=2.02
29	-0.03	p=0.95	t=0.07	0.64	p=0.18	t=1.64
30	0.40	p=0.37	t=0.98	0.23	p=0.66	t=0.47
31	0.36	p=0.43	t=0.85	0.13	p=0.80	t=0.27

Table E-7: Correlations of performance Measures With All Team Leader Survey (TLS) Items

Item	Correlation with:					
	BRP			BPCS		
Dimension						
Leadership	-0.49	p=0.26	t=1.26	-0.75	p=0.08	t=2.29
Empowerment	-0.19	p=0.69	t=0.43	-0.29	p=0.58	t=0.61
Self-management	-0.04	p=0.94	t=0.08	-0.59	p=0.21	t=1.47
Coping	-0.24	p=0.60	t=0.56	-0.12	p=0.82	t=0.25
Learning-others	0.03	p=0.95	t=0.06	-0.40	p=0.43	t=0.88
Learning-own	0.30	p=0.51	t=0.71	-0.10	p=0.85	t=0.20
Total	-0.07	p=0.88	t=0.16	-0.46	p=0.36	t=1.02

Table E-7 (continued)

Time 2						
		Correlation with:				
Item	BRP			BPCS		
Dimension						
Leadership	-0.17	p=0.71	t=0.39	0.29	p=0.58	t=0.60
Empowerment	0.07	p=0.88	t=0.15	0.19	p=0.71	t=0.39
Self-management	0.22	p=0.64	t=0.49	0.39	p=0.44	t=0.86
Coping	-0.04	p=0.93	t=0.10	0.90	p=0.01	t=4.19
Learning-others	0.22	p=0.64	t=0.50	0.28	p=0.59	t=0.59
Learning-own	0.29	p=0.53	t=0.68	0.57	p=0.24	t=1.38
Total	0.18	p=0.70	t=0.41	0.60	p=0.21	t=1.48

FACTOR SUMMARY

Table E-8: Correlation of Performance Measures With Team Leader Survey

(TLS) Factors

Time 1

Factors	Correlation with:					
	BRP			BPCS		
1	0.32	p=0.49	t=0.75	0.47	p=0.35	t=1.06
2	-0.14	p=0.76	t=0.32	0.29	p=0.57	t=0.61
Total	0.25	p=0.59	t=0.57	0.51	p=0.30	t=1.19

Time 2

Factors	Correlation with:					
	BRP			BPCS		
1	0.11	p=0.81	t=0.25	-0.64	p=0.17	t=1.66
2	-0.18	p=0.70	t=0.41	0.33	p=0.52	t=0.70
Total	0.07	p=0.88	t=0.16	-0.49	p=0.32	t=1.14

Table E-9: Descriptive Statistics for Self-managing Team (SMT) Leader Survey

Item	Mean	S.D.
Encourage open communication among team members	4.78	0.44
Identify problems teams are avoiding	3.44	0.73
Obtain resources for team members	4.00	0.71
Develop a climate of teamwork	4.11	0.78
Foster smooth team interaction	4.44	0.53
Change course to take advantage of opportunities	3.89	0.78
Listen to team members	4.78	0.44
Solve team problems on my own	3.22	0.83
Establish priorities for the team	2.67	0.87
Encourage team members to manage themselves	4.11	0.78
Address interpersonal problems on a one-to-one basis	2.00	0.87
Cope with uncertainty	3.78	0.67
Keep information to myself	4.22	1.09
Anticipate potential problems for the team	3.33	0.71
Help teams to meet schedule requirements	4.44	0.73
Make decisions for the team	3.56	0.73
Develop a climate of personal growth for team members	3.67	0.71
Stick to the original plan when the unexpected occurs	3.78	0.97
Give feedback to team members	4.00	0.71
Focus on one side of an issue	4.33	0.71
Pay attention to detail	4.11	0.78
Influence people to follow the rules	2.11	0.60
Develop solutions that capitalize on the differences among team members	3.33	0.71
Present alternative ideas to team members	4.22	0.67
Communicate thoughts clearly	4.33	1.00
Observe own behaviors	3.11	1.05
Improve the way the team operates	3.56	0.53
Encourage team members to develop new skills	3.89	1.05
Rely on the most knowledgeable team members for input	2.89	1.36
Can handle only one assignment at a time	4.22	0.97
Neglect to communicate customer requirements	4.33	0.87

Table E-9 (continued)

Item	Mean	S.D.
Attend to nonverbal cues	3.33	1.00
Overlook opportunities to coordinate activities between teams	4.11	0.78
Encourage team members to monitor own performance	3.67	0.87
Work through conflicts	3.78	0.83
Respond to unanticipated changes	4.44	0.53
Dimension		
Communication	26.44	3.17
Thinking	20.78	2.33
Administration	22.89	1.90
Leadership	21.44	2.07
Interpersonal	20.11	2.37
Flexibility	24.33	2.55
Total	136.00	11.11

Note: N=9 (9 teams = 118 members)

Table E-10: Self-managing Team (SMT) Leader Survey

Time 1

Item	Correlation with:					
	BRP			BPCS		
1	0.45	p=0.31	t=1.14	-0.11	p=0.83	t=0.23
2	0.13	p=0.78	t=0.29	0.24	p=0.65	t=0.50
3	0.45	p=0.31	t=1.14	0.20	p=0.70	t=0.41
4	0.45	p=0.32	t=1.12	-0.47	p=0.35	t=1.06
5	0.12	p=0.80	t=0.26	-0.44	p=0.38	t=0.99
6	-0.39	p=0.39	t=0.94	-0.06	p=0.91	t=0.12
7	0.45	p=0.31	t=1.14	-0.11	p=0.83	t=0.23
8	0.20	p=0.66	t=0.47	-0.38	p=0.46	t=0.81
9	-0.09	p=0.84	t=0.21	0.23	p=0.66	t=0.48
10	-0.35	p=0.45	t=0.82	-0.47	p=0.35	t=1.06
11	-0.29	p=0.52	t=0.69	0.44	p=0.38	t=0.99
12	0.26	p=0.57	t=0.61	-0.31	p=0.54	t=0.66
13	0.61	p=0.15	t=1.70	0.87	p=0.02	t=3.57
14	-0.09	p=0.84	t=0.21	0.24	p=0.65	t=0.50
15	0.16	p=0.74	t=0.36	-0.11	p=0.83	t=0.23
16	-0.06	p=0.91	t=0.12	0.24	p=0.65	t=0.50
17	0.06	p=0.90	t=0.13	-0.73	p=0.10	t=2.15

Table E-10 (continued)

Item	Correlation with:					
	BRP			BPCS		
18	0.09	p=0.86	t=0.19	0.47	p=0.35	t=1.05
19	0.30	p=0.52	t=0.70	0.20	p=0.70	t=0.41
20	0.34	p=0.45	t=0.82	0.73	p=0.10	t=2.15
21	0.54	p=0.21	t=1.45	0.15	p=0.77	t=0.31
22	-0.28	p=0.54	t=0.65	0.11	p=0.83	t=0.23
23	-0.08	p=0.87	t=0.18	-0.99	p=0.00	t=18.07
24	0.02	p=0.97	t=0.05	0.26	p=0.62	t=0.54
25	0.04	p=0.93	t=0.09	0.22	p=0.68	t=0.45
26	-0.29	p=0.52	t=0.69	-0.52	p=0.29	t=1.23
27	0.45	p=0.31	t=1.14	-0.44	p=0.38	t=0.99
28	0.43	p=0.34	t=1.06	-0.51	p=0.31	t=1.17
29	-0.20	p=0.67	t=0.46	0.64	p=0.17	t=1.69
30	-0.41	p=0.36	t=1.01	0.50	p=0.31	t=1.16
31	-0.53	p=0.22	t=1.39	0.67	p=0.15	t=1.79
32	-0.05	p=0.91	t=0.12	-0.49	p=0.32	t=1.13
33	0.01	p=0.99	t=0.02	0.59	p=0.22	t=1.44
34	-0.84	p=0.02	t=3.52	-0.59	p=0.21	t=1.48
35	-0.11	p=0.81	t=0.25	-0.69	p=0.13	t=1.88
36	-0.74	p=0.06	t=2.47	-0.59	p=0.21	t=1.48

Table E-11: Correlations of Performance Measures With All Self-managing Team Leader (SMT) Survey Items

Time 2

Item	Correlation with:					
	BRP			BPCS		
1	0.54	p=0.21	t=1.44	0.13	p=0.80	t=0.27
2	0.36	p=0.43	t=0.87	-0.13	p=0.80	t=0.27
3	0.54	p=0.21	t=1.44	-0.07	p=0.89	t=0.14
4	0.49	p=0.26	t=1.26	-0.07	p=0.89	t=0.14
5	0.27	p=0.56	t=0.62	0.30	p=0.57	t=0.62
6	-0.15	p=0.74	t=0.35	0.67	p=0.15	t=1.80
7	0.54	p=0.21	t=1.44	0.13	p=0.80	t=0.27
8	0.09	p=0.84	t=0.21	0.42	p=0.41	t=0.92
9	-0.10	p=0.83	t=0.22	-0.58	p=0.23	t=1.43
10	-0.04	p=0.93	t=0.09	0.14	p=0.79	t=0.28
11	-0.22	p=0.63	t=0.51	-0.30	p=0.57	t=0.62
12	0.61	p=0.15	t=1.70	0.45	p=0.37	t=1.01
13	0.55	p=0.20	t=1.47	-0.15	p=0.77	t=0.31
14	0.23	p=0.62	t=0.52	0.97	p=0.00	t=7.70
15	-0.03	p=0.95	t=0.06	0.13	p=0.80	t=0.27
16	-0.05	p=0.91	t=0.12	-0.13	p=0.80	t=0.27
17	0.21	p=0.65	t=0.48	0.07	p=0.89	t=0.14

Table E-11 (continued)

Item	Correlation with:					
	BRP			BPCS		
18	0.24	t=0.56	p=0.60	-0.40	t=0.88	p=0.43
19	0.41	t=0.99	p=0.37	0.52	t=1.23	p=0.29
20	0.38	t=0.92	p=0.40	-0.07	t=0.14	p=0.89
21	0.48	t=1.22	p=0.28	0.36	t=0.77	p=0.49
22	-0.50	t=1.29	p=0.25	-0.13	t=0.27	p=0.80
23	0.14	t=0.33	p=0.76	-0.13	t=0.27	p=0.80
24	-0.13	t=0.28	p=0.79	-0.29	t=0.60	p=0.58
25	-0.03	t=0.08	p=0.94	0.18	t=0.36	p=0.74
26	0.06	t=0.13	p=0.90	0.64	t=1.66	p=0.17
27	0.54	t=1.44	p=0.21	0.30	t=0.62	p=0.57
28	0.64	t=1.88	p=0.12	0.50	t=1.16	p=0.31
29	-0.29	t=0.67	p=0.53	-0.08	t=0.15	p=0.89
30	-0.27	t=0.64	p=0.55	0.64	t=1.66	p=0.17
31	-0.43	t=1.06	p=0.34	0.40	t=0.88	p=0.43
32	-0.13	t=0.30	p=0.78	-0.93	t=5.25	p=0.01
33	0.19	t=0.44	p=0.68	0.84	t=3.04	p=0.04
34	-0.60	t=1.66	p=0.16	0.66	t=1.76	p=0.15
35	0.22	t=0.51	p=0.63	0.24	t=0.49	p=0.65
36	-0.47	t=1.19	p=0.29	0.66	t=1.76	p=0.15

Table E-12: Correlations of Performance measures with Self-managing Team (SMT) Leader Survey Dimensions

Time 1

Item	Correlation with:					
	BRP			BPCS		
Dimension						
Communication	0.29	p=0.52	t=0.68	0.56	p=0.25	t=1.36
Thinking	0.02	p=0.96	t=0.05	-0.75	p=0.08	t=2.29
Administration	0.52	p=0.23	t=1.35	0.37	p=0.47	t=0.80
Leadership	-0.18	p=0.70	t=0.40	-0.65	p=0.16	t=1.70
Interpersonal	-0.22	p=0.63	t=0.51	-0.37	p=0.48	t=0.78
Flexibility	-0.32	p=0.49	t=0.74	0.28	p=0.59	t=0.58
Total	0.01	p=0.99	t=0.02	0.05	p=0.93	t=0.10

Table E-12 (continued)

Time 2

Item	Correlation with:					
	BRP			BPCS		
Dimension						
Communication	0.32	p=0.48	t=0.77	0.26	p=0.62	t=0.54
Thinking	0.29	p=0.53	t=0.68	0.29	p=0.58	t=0.60
Administration	0.54	p=0.21	t=1.45	0.25	p=0.63	t=0.52
Leadership	0.08	p=0.87	t=0.18	0.35	p=0.49	t=0.75
Interpersonal	0.03	p=0.95	t=0.07	0.00	p=1.00	t=0.00
Flexibility	-0.05	p=0.92	t=0.10	0.47	p=0.35	t=1.05
Total	0.24	p=0.61	t=0.55	0.33	p=0.52	t=0.70

Table E-13: Correlation of Performance Measures with Self-Managing Team (SMT) Leader Survey Factors

Time 1

Factors	Correlation with:					
	BRP			BPCS		
1	0.53	p=0.22	t=1.39	0.37	p=0.47	t=0.80
2	-0.12	p=0.80	t=0.27	-0.72	p=0.10	t=2.09
Total	0.56	p=0.19	t=1.51	0.12	p=0.82	t=0.24

Time 2

Factors	Correlation with:					
	BRP			BPCS		
1	0.33	p=0.47	t=0.78	-0.48	p=0.33	t=1.10
2	-0.13	p=0.78	t=0.29	-0.17	p=0.74	t=0.35
Total	0.33	p=0.47	t=0.79	-0.49	p=0.33	t=1.12

Bibliography

Bales, R. F. 1958. Task roles and social roles in problem-solving groups. In E. E. Maccoby, T. M. Newcomb, and E. L. Hartley (Eds.), *Readings in social psychology*. (3rd ed.) New York: Holt, Rinehart & Winston.

Bandura, A. 1969. *Principles of behavior modification*. New York: Holt, Rinehart & Winston.

———— 1977. *Social learning theory*. Englewood Cliffs. Prentice-Hall.

———— 1978. The self system in reciprocal determinism. *American Psychologist*, 33: 344-58.

———— 1986. *Social foundations of thought and action: A social cognitive theory*. Englewood Cliffs, N.J.: Prentice-Hall.

Beekun, R. I. 1989. Assessing the effectiveness of socio-technical interventions: Antidote or fad? *Human Relations*, 42(10), 877-97.

Beyerlein, M. 1995, Fall. Measuring team performance: The literature. *Work teams newsletter*, Vol. 5, no. 3, University of North Texas.

Beyerlein, M. and Johnson, D. (editors). 1994. *Advances in interdisciplinary studies of work teams*. Greenwich: JAI Press.

Borg, W. R. and Gall, M. D. 1989. *Educational research: An introduction* (5th. ed.). New York: Longman.

Burns, T. and Stalker, G. M. 1961. *The Management of Innovation*. London: Tavistock.

Burress, A. 1992. *Development of a model of leadership for self-managed teams in a greenfield environment*. (Master's thesis, University of North Texas, 1992, MicS 160 no. 6788).

———— 1993. *Leader behavior for self-managing teams.* Unpublished manuscript, University of North Texas at Denton.

———— 1994. *SMT leader survey*. King of Prussia, Pa. Organization Design and Development.

Caminiti, S. What team leaders need to know. *Fortune,* February 20, 1995.

Cherns, A. B. 1976. The principles of socio-technical design. *Human Relations,* vol. 29: 783-92.

Cohen, S. 1993. *Designing effective self-managing work teams.* Report no. G93-9 (229). Los Angeles: Center for Effective Organizations, The University of Southern California.

———— 1994. Designing effective self-managing work teams. In M. M. Beyerlein and D. A. Johnson (Eds.), *Advances in interdisciplinary studies of work teams.* Greenwich, Conn.: JAI Press. 67-102.

Cohen, S. G. and Ledford, G. E., Jr. 1991. *The effectiveness of self-managing teams: A quasi-experiment.* (Report No. G901-6) Los Angeles: University of Southern California.

Cummings, G. T. 1978. Self-regulating work groups: A socio-technical synthesis. *Academy of Management Review.* no. 3, July: 625-34.

Cummings, G. T. and Srivastva, S. 1977. *Management of work: A socio-technical systems approach.* San Diego: University Associates.

Dumaine, B. The trouble with teams. *Fortune.* September 5, 1994.

———— Who needs a boss? *Fortune.* May 7, 1990.

Eccles, Robert G. 1992 *Beyond the hype.* Boston: Harvard Business School Press.

Fields, M. 1984. Exploratory data analysis in organizational research. In Bateman, T. S. and Ferris, G. R. (Eds.). *Method and analysis in organizational research.* Reston: Prentice-Hall.

Fisher, K. 1993. *Leading self-directed work teams.* New York: McGraw Hill.

Fotilas, P. N. 1981. Semi-autonomous work groups: An alternative in organizing production work? *Management Review.* vol. 70: 50-54.

French, W. L. and Bell, C. H. Jr., 1984. A history of organization development in *Organization development: Behavioral science interventions for organization development.* 3rd Ed. Englewood Cliffs, N.J.: Prentice-Hall.

Freire, P. 1970. *Pedagogy of the oppressed.* New York: The Seabury Press.

Galbraith, J. R.1973. *Designing complex organizations.* Reading, Mass.: Addison-Wesley.

———— 1977. *Organization design.* Reading, Mass: Addison-Wesley.

———— 1995. *Designing organizations.* San Francisco: Jossey-Bass.

Glaser, R. (Ed.). 1992. *Classic readings in self-managing teamwork.* King of Prussia, Pa.: Organization Design and Development.

———— 1991. *Facilitating Adult Learning in Semi-Autonomous Work Groups.* Dissertation: Teachers College, Columbia University.

Goodman, P. S.; Devadas, R.; and Hughson, T. G. 1988. Groups and productivity: Analyzing the effectiveness of self-managing teams. In J. P.

Campbell, R. J. Campbell, and Associates (Eds.), *Productivity in Organizations*, San Francisco: 295-327.

Hackman, J. R. and Oldham, G. R. 1980. *Work redesign.* Reading, Mass: Addison-Wesley.

Hackman, J. R. 1985. Doing research that makes a difference. In E. E. Lawler III, A. M. Mohrman, Jr., S. A. Mohrman, G. E. Ledford, T. G. Cummings and Associates (Eds.). *Doing research that is useful for theory and practice.* San Francisco: Jossey-Bass.

———— 1986. The psychology of self-management in organizations. In M. S. Pallak and R. O. Perloff, (Eds). *Psychology and work: Productivity, change, and employment.* Washington, D.C.: American Psychological Association.

Hackman, J. R. and Walton, R. E. 1986. Leading groups in organizations. In P. S. Goodman (Ed.), *Designing effective work groups.* San Francisco: Jossey-Bass.

Hackman, J. R., (Ed.). 1990. *Groups that work (and those that don't).* San Francisco: Jossey-Bass.

Hemphill, J. K. 1950. *Leader Behavior Description.* Columbus, Ohio: Ohio State University Press.

Kemp, N. J.; Wall, T. D.; Clegg, C. W.; and Cordery, J. L. 1983. Autonomous work groups in a greenfield site: A comparative study. *Journal of Occupational Psychology,* vol. 56: 271-88.

Ketchum, L. D. and Trist, E. 1992. *All teams are not created equal.* Newbury Park: Sage Publications.

Latham, G. P. and Saari, L. M. 1979. Application of social learning theory to training supervisors through behavioral modeling. *Journal of Applied Psychology*, June, 239-46.

Lawler, E. E. 1978. The new plant revolution. *Organization Dynamics*, 6, 2-12.

———— 1986. *High involvement management.* San Francisco: Jossey-Bass.

———— 1987. Transformation from control to involvement. In R. H. Kilmann, T. J. Covin, and Associates, *Corporate Transformation.* San Francisco: Jossey-Bass.

———— 1992 *The ultimate advantage: Creating the high-involvement organization.* San Francisco: Jossey-Bass.

———— 1996. *From the ground up: Six principles for building the new logic corporation.* San Francisco: Jossey-Bass.

Lawler, E., Ledford, G. and Mohrman, M. 1994. *Conference on designing team-based organizations.* October 13, 1994. Center for Effective Organizations, University of Southern California.

Lawler, E.; Mohrman, S.; and Ledford, G. 1995. *Creating high performance organizations*. San Francisco: Jossey-Bass.

Lawrence, P. R. and Lorsch, J. W. 1969. *Organization and environment*. Homewood, Ill.: Richard D. Irwin, Inc.

Lewin, K. 1951. *Field theory in the social sciences*. New York: Harper and Row.

McMillan, J. H. and Schumacher, S. 1989. *Research in education*. New York: Harper Collins Publishers.

Manz, C. C. and Sims, H. P. Jr., 1980. Self-management as a substitute for leadership: A social learning theory perspective. *Academy of Management Review*; 5, 361-67.

———— 1984. Searching for the "unleader:" Organizational member views on leading self-managing groups. *Human Relations*, 37, 409-24.

Manz, C. C. 1986. Leading self-managed groups: A conceptual analysis of paradox. *Economic and industrial democracy*, 7; 141-65.

———— 1986. Self-leadership: Toward an expanded theory of self-influence processes in organizations. *Academy of management review*. 11: 585-600.

Manz, C. C. and Sims, H. P. 1986. Leading self-managed groups: A conceptual analysis of a paradox. *Economic and Industrial Democracy*. 7: 141-65.

Manz, C. C. and Sims, H. P., Jr. 1987. Leading workers to lead themselves: The external leadership of self-managing work teams. *Administrative Science Quarterly*, vol. 32: 106-128.

———— 1989. *SuperLeadership*: New York: Berkeley Books.

Manz, C. C., Keating, D. E. and Donnellon, A. 1990. Preparing for an organizational change to self-management: The managerial transition. *Organizational Dynamics*. 19 (2), 15-26.

———— 1990. *Becoming a SuperLeader*. King of Prussia, Pa.: Organization Design and Development.

———— (1993). *Business without bosses*. New York: John Wiley & Sons, Inc.

Marrow, A. 1969. *The practical theorist*. New York: Basic Books.

Marsick, V. J. (Ed.). 1987. *Learning in the workplace*. New York: Croom Helm.

Merriam, S. B., and Caffarella, R. S. 1991. San Francisco: *Learning in adulthood.* San Francisco: Jossey-Bass.

Mezirow, J. and Associates 1990. *Fostering critical reflection in adulthood: A guide to transformative and emancipatory education*. San Francisco: Jossey-Bass.

Mills, P. K. 1983. Self-management: Its control and relationship to other organizational properties. *Academy of Management Review*, 8: 445-53.

Mohrman, S. A. and Cummings, T. G. 1989. *Self-designing organizations: Learning how to create high performance.* Reading, Mass.: Addison-Wesley.

Mohrman, S. A. 1994. Letter from the Center for Effective Organizations to Friends of the CEO (sponsor organizations).

Mohrman, S.; Mohrman, A.; and Cohen, S. 1994. Organizing knowledge work systems. *Designing team based organizations.* Conference conducted at the Center for Effective Organizations, University of Southern California, October 13, 1994.

Mohrman, S. and Cohen, S. 1994. When people get out of the box: New attachments to co-workers. *The changing nature of work.* San Francisco: Jossey-Bass.

Mohrman, S. and Mohrman, A. 1994. *Large-scale organizational change as learning: Creating team-based organizations.* Paper presented at corporate change: an international research conference, The University of New South Wales. August, 1994.

Nadler, D. What team leaders need to know. In Caminiti, S. *Fortune.* February 20, 1995.

Nadler, D. A.; Gerstein, M. S.; and Shaw, R. B. 1992. *Organizational architecture: Designs for changing organizations.* San Francisco: Jossey-Bass.

Nadler, D. A. and Tushman, M. L.1988. *Strategic organization design.* Glenview, Ill.: Scott, Foresman.

Parsons, T. 1960. *Structure and process in modern societies,* New York: John Wiley & Sons.

Pasmore, W. A., and Sherwood, J. J. (Eds.). 1978. *Sociotechnical systems: A sourcebook.* San Diego: University Associates, Inc.

Pearce, J. A. II and Ravlin, E. C. 1987. The design and activation of self-regulating work groups. *Human Relations.* vol. 40: 751-82.

Peters, T. 1987. *Thriving on chaos: Handbook for management revolution.* New York: Alfred Knopf.

Ranney, J. M. and Jamieson, K. 1986. Bringing sociotechnical systems from the factory to the office. *National Productivity Review,* vol. 5: 124-33.

Sashkin, M. 1985. *Trainer guide: Leader behavior questionnaire.* King of Prussia, Pa.: Organization Design and Development.

Sashkin, M. and Glaser, R. 1990. *How to choose a learning instrument for training and development: Ten criteria.* King of Prussia, PA.: Organization Design and Development.

Sashkin, M. and Rosenbach, W. E. 1993. A new leadership paradigm. In Rosenbach, W. E. and Taylor, R. L. (Eds.) *Contemporary issues in leadership.* Boulder: Westview Press.

Schein, E. 1993. On dialogue, culture, and organizational learning. *Organizational Dynamics,* vol. 22.

Senge, P. 1990. *The fifth discipline: The art and practice of the learning organization.* New York: Doubleday.

Senge, P.; Kleiner, A.; Roberts, C.; and Ross, R.; Smith, B. 1994. *The fifth discipline fieldbook.* New York: Doubleday.

Siegel, S. 1956. *Nonparametric statistics for the behavioral sciences.* New York: McGraw Hill.

Sims, H. and Lorenzi, P. 1992. *The new leadership paradigm.* Newbury Park: Sage Publications.

Tabachnick, B. G. and Fidell, L. S. 1989. *Using multivariate statistics.* New York: Harper & Row.

Taylor, F. W. 1911. *The principles of scientific management.* New York: Harper Collins.

Trist, E. L. and Bamforth, R. 1951. Some social and psychological consequences of the long wall method of coal-getting. *Human Relations.* vol. 4: 3-38.

Tubbs. S. L. 1994. The historical roots of self-managing work teams in the twentieth century: An annotated bibliography. In M. M. Beyerlein and D. A. Johnson (Eds.), *Advances in interdisciplinary studies of work teams.* 39-66. Greenwich: JAI Press.

Von Bertalanffy, L. 1950. The theory of open systems in physics and biology. *Science.* 3: 23-29.

——— 1955. General systems theory. *Main currents in modern thought.* vol. 11: 4-76.

Walton, R. E. 1985. From control to commitment in the workplace. *Harvard Business Review.* 63: 77-84.

——— 1975. The diffusion of new work structures: Explaining why success didn't take. *Organizational Dynamics.* Winter: 3-22.

Watkins, K. E. and Marsick, V. J. 1993. *Sculpting the learning organization.* San Francisco: Jossey Bass.

Webster's collegiate dictionary (9th ed.). 1984. Springfield, Mass.: Merriam-Webster.

Weber, M. 1947. *The theory of social and economic organization.* New York: Free Press.

Weisbord, M. 1987. *Productive workplaces.* San Francisco: Jossey-Bass.

Wellins, R. S. 1990. *Self-directed teams: A study of current practice.* Survey report. Pittsburgh: Development Dimensions International.

Wellins, R. S.; Byham, W. C.; and Wilson, J. M. 1991. *Empowered teams.* San Francisco: Jossey-Bass.

Index

adult learning, 11, 22-25
autonomous work team, 14

Bandura, 10-11, 15, 66
Beyerlein, 4, 20
BPCS, 9, 33, 38, 59
BRP, 9, 33, 38, 59
Burress, 7, 11, 18-20, 31, 38, 45-46, 62
Business Planning and Control System (BPCS), 9, 33
Business Resources Planning (BRP), 9, 33

Caminiti, 17
Cohen, 5, 6, 10, 11, 15, 20, 29
Cross, 22
cross-functional teams, 4
Cummings, 11, 13

dialogue, 24
Dumaine, 15

empowered leadership, 10, 63
empowered teams, 4

Freire, 22, 23

Galbraith, 4, 5, 13, 28
general systems, 11
Glaser, 6, 7, 10-11, 17-18, 20-24, 42, 62, 65
Goodman, Devadas, & Hughson, 5, 20

Hackman, 10, 63
high performance work systems, 13

Jarvis, 22

Knowles, 22
Knox, 22
Kraft, 42, 46, 49

lateral organizations, 3
Lawler, 4, 8, 13, 15
leadership, 5, 7, 9, 17, 24, 62-63, 65-66
learning organizations, 24
Ledford, 6, 10, 29
Lorenzi, 62

Manz, 10
Manz and Sims, 4-6, 8, 11, 20, 28, 62
McClusky, 22